# The Self-Help Industry

# The Self-Help Industry

### By

## Dr Bruno De Oliveira

**iff**

**IFF
BOOKS**

London, UK
Washington, DC, USA

# CollectiveInk

First published by iff Books, 2025
iff Books is an imprint of Collective Ink Ltd.,
Unit 11, Shepperton House, 89 Shepperton Road, London, N1 3DF
office@collectiveinkbooks.com
www.collectiveinkbooks.com
www.iff-books.com

For distributor details and how to order please visit the 'Ordering' section on our website.

Text copyright: Dr Bruno De Oliveira 2024

ISBN: 978 1 80341 980 0 (Paperback)
978 1 80341 989 3 (ebook)
Library of Congress Control Number: 2024949182

A CIP catalogue record for this book is available from the British Library.

Design: Lapiz Digital Services

UK: Printed and bound by CPI Group (UK) Ltd, Croydon, CR0 4YY
Printed in North America by CPI GPS partners

We operate a distinctive and ethical publishing philosophy in all areas of our business, from our global network of authors to production and worldwide distribution.

# Contents

# Foreword

The 2008 comedy *Yes Man*, starring Jim Carrey, took a playful dive into embracing life's opportunities with a simple, powerful word: "Yes". The premise is deceptively simple – what if you said "yes" to every opportunity that came your way? For Carl Allen (Jim Carrey), a downtrodden bank loan officer stuck in a rut of routine and negativity, this radical life-changing decision leads to an unexpected and often hilarious transformation. But while the movie's message – that we should be open to new experiences and that good things can come from "giving it a go" – resonates with the audience, it also invites a critical examination. In particular, *Yes Man* offers a curious exploration of the fine line between optimism and absurdity and the potential dangers of taking the concept of saying "yes" too literally.

At its heart, *Yes Man* is a comedic celebration of life's possibilities, urging viewers to break free from self-imposed limitations and embrace the unknown. Carl's life is a mundane carousel of missed opportunities, broken friendships, and a general lack of enthusiasm. When he stumbles upon a self-help seminar led by the charismatic Terrence Bundley (played by Terence Stamp), Carl is indoctrinated into the world of "Yes", a philosophy that mandates saying yes to everything – no matter how ludicrous or outlandish. The results are immediate and dramatic: Carl's life turns from the monotonous to the miraculous, as he suddenly finds himself learning Korean, taking flying lessons, and rescuing strangers from the brink of despair. The message seems clear – by saying yes, Carl is living life to the fullest, experiencing things he never imagined possible.

On the surface, the movie's central message is appealing. After all, life is full of missed opportunities, and how often do we look back with regret on the things we didn't do rather than the things we did? *Yes Man* taps into a universal human truth: fear of failure, rejection, or the unknown can keep us from trying new things, but without trying, we'll never know what we might have missed. The film suggests that by taking risks and opening ourselves up to new experiences, we can transform our lives profoundly and positively. But here's the catch – while the movie gleefully promotes the idea of saying yes to everything, it glosses over the potential consequences of such an approach. The film portrays Carl's initial reluctance to say yes as the root of all his problems. Yet, it quickly becomes apparent that saying yes to everything isn't a foolproof strategy. For every beautiful new experience Carl gains – such as meeting the quirky and free-spirited Allison (Zooey Deschanel), who introduces him to a vibrant, more spontaneous way of living – there's an equally absurd or downright dangerous outcome. Whether it's agreeing to bungee jump off a bridge, saying yes to a homeless man's request that depletes his gas tank and wallet, or ending up in a bar brawl, Carl's enthusiastic "yes" responses often lead him into dangerous situations that would make any reasonable person pause for thought.

The film's comedy hinges on the increasingly ridiculous scenarios Carl finds himself in, but these serve as more than just fodder for laughs; they subtly critique the unexamined embrace of perpetual positivity. The "yes" philosophy, taken to its extreme, becomes less about living life fully and more about abandoning critical thinking. Saying yes to everything without considering the context, appropriateness, or consequences quickly turns into escapism. One of the film's underlying ironies is that while Carl's life initially improves due to him saying yes, things don't take long to spiral out of control. The movie acknowledges that unchecked positivity or a refusal to say no can lead to poor decisions and even harm to oneself and others. It's a far cry from the original self-help sentiment, which is supposed to encourage growth and empowerment. Instead, it suggests a cautionary tale: the idea that one-size-fits-all solutions, especially in self-improvement, can be just as limiting as the barriers they aim to dismantle.

The character arc in *Yes Man* also demonstrates that the benefits of saying yes are not in the act itself but in the balance it brings to Carl's previously stunted life. Initially, Carl's problem was not just that he was saying no but that he was doing so out of fear and habit rather than discernment. The film's resolution, where Carl learns to say no, when necessary, underscores a critical aspect of personal growth: the need for balance. True empowerment comes not from saying yes or no but from the ability to make thoughtful choices. This brings us to another significant point of critique – how *Yes Man* skirts the many possibilities of decision-making in favour of a simplistic, if entertaining, narrative. Life's challenges and opportunities do not exist in a vacuum; they are influenced by context, timing, and personal readiness. The movie's premise that good things happen when you open yourself to the world holds some truth, but it dangerously simplifies making meaningful life changes. A world where one perpetually says yes to everything isn't just unrealistic – it's unsustainable. The romantic subplot between Carl and Allison also deserves a closer look. While their relationship flourishes due to Carl's newfound openness, it also exemplifies the potential downsides of the "yes" philosophy. Allison is portrayed as the quintessential "free spirit", whose charm lies in her spontaneity and love for the unpredictable. However, the film never truly addresses whether Carl's yes-man approach is sustainable in the long run.

Ultimately, *Yes Man* offers a fun and humorous exploration of personal growth and the importance of stepping outside one's comfort zone. However, it also serves as a reminder of the pitfalls of adopting life philosophies wholesale. The film's central message is that good things can come from "giving it a go" and can be valuable. Still, this must be tempered with the understanding that not all experiences are beneficial and not all opportunities are worth pursuing. The key takeaway, perhaps, is that while saying yes can indeed open doors, it's the wisdom to know when to say no that ultimately leads to a balanced and fulfilling life. In this way, *Yes Man* can reflect the broader cultural obsession with positivity and self-improvement, often found in the self-help genre. Much like Carl's initial overzealous embrace of "yes", the self-help industry frequently promotes overly simplistic solutions to complicated life issues, encouraging readers to believe that happiness and success are just a few affirmations or positive thoughts away. Yet, as Carl's journey illustrates, actual growth and contentment come not from unthinkingly following any one mantra but from learning to navigate the shades of grey in life's many decisions.

# Introduction

A very wealthy "friend" from university was the kind of chap who, well into his 40s, was still pondering the universe's great mysteries by using crystals, salt lamps and cosmic energy. He had fallen down the rabbit hole of self-help books, spurred on by a particularly popular life coach with a suspiciously glowing white smile. Despite coming from a wealthy family, he was convinced that the universe was plotting his ultimate success. All he had to do was trust in its infinite wisdom and step out of his comfort zone. Now, most people might start with something manageable – maybe a new hobby like *Couch to 5k* or knitting. But not my Uni friend. No, he decided that the universe wanted him to become a surfer. The closest he'd ever come to a surfboard was watching a documentary on Hawaiian beaches while eating carrot sticks at home on his sofa. But convinced that the universe would transform him into a wave-riding guru, he booked a trip to Cornwall, the surfing capital of the UK. He arrived at the beach, slathered himself in organic Factor 50 sun cream and put on a wetsuit that was a size too small. But he was undeterred. After all, the book had assured him that the universe would provide. It did not mention anything about balance, strength, or the basic knowledge of how to surf, but details like that seemed trivial to him. The universe would take care of it. He paddled out, wobbling on his board but filled with optimism.

The first wave came, and with all the grace of a giraffe on roller skates, he stood up for about 0.3 seconds before the surfboard decided it had had enough of this universe nonsense. Vengefully, it flipped and whacked him square in the face. It was a proper wallop. He went down faster than the British pound after Brexit. When he surfaced, he looked around, dazed, blood trickling from his now crooked nose, and thought, "Ah, perhaps this is the universe's way of teaching me humility." But there was no time for astrological reflections because the waves kept coming. Thankfully, the lifeguards on duty were not as optimistic about the universe's goodwill as he was. They spotted him struggling and swiftly came to the rescue, dragging him back to shore where a small crowd had gathered to see him with a face now resembling a Picasso painting, dribbling saltwater and nursing what would later be confirmed as a broken nose and cheekbone. Sitting on the beach, clutching an ice pack to his face, he finally conceded that perhaps the universe would not make him the next Kelly Slater. He returned home with a few cracked bones, a dented ego, and maybe a newfound respect for the sea. His surfing career ended as quickly as it had begun. As for the universe, it's probably still laughing as he went on an ice bath trip to find himself. In all fairness, ice seems to be suitable for the injuries he gained.

The self-help industry, a global behemoth worth over $11 billion, is a panacea for individuals' myriad personal and societal challenges (Salerno, 2006). A report by The Business Research Company (2024) estimates that the personal development market size has grown strongly in recent years. It was predicted to grow from $48.11 billion in 2023 to $51.06 billion in 2024 at a compound annual growth rate (CAGR) of 6.1%. From improving self-esteem to achieving financial success, the genre claims to offer tools for all aspects of life, drawing in an audience eager to find solutions to their existential dilemmas. This vast industry, encompassing books, seminars, online courses, and personal coaching, promises empowerment, transformation, and the elusive "better self" (McGee, 2005). However, beneath this veneer of positivity lies the "Self-Help Paradox" – the tension between the allure of self-improvement and the often superficial, commodified nature of the solutions offered. This paradox necessitates critically examining the self-help industry to test its promises and understand its pervasive influence and the socio-cultural dynamics that sustain it. The allure of self-help is deeply rooted in the cultural fabric of Western societies, particularly in the context of neoliberalism and the emphasis on individualism (Illouz, 2008). In an era where personal responsibility is valorised, the idea that one can "fix" oneself resonates powerfully. Self-help books like *How to Win Friends and Influence People* and *The 7 Habits of Highly Effective People* have become modern-day holy scripts to life, offering practical advice for personal and professional success. These "holy texts", as well as countless others, reinforce the notion that individuals possess the innate capacity to overcome obstacles, provided they adopt the right mindset and behaviours.

Self-help's appeal is amplified by its accessibility and the simplicity of its messages. In a world where having to be successful often leads to paralysis, the straightforward, actionable advice found in self-help literature provides a comforting sense of control (Starker, 2002). This industry capitalises on the human desire for quick fixes and the belief that happiness and success are within reach if only one follows the prescribed steps or pillars. The language of self-help is inherently seductive, filled with anecdotes of triumph over adversity, and imbued with the optimism that change is not only possible but inevitable. Important lessons such as those found in the myth of Sisyphus teach us the importance of resilience and perseverance in the face of adversity. Sisyphus was condemned to an eternity of ceaseless toil, yet he continued to push the boulder up the hill despite it rolling back down each time. Then there is the myth of Hercules, the son of Zeus, the king of the gods, and a mortal woman named Alcmene. Hercules was known for his incredible strength and endurance, which he used to complete twelve impossible tasks known as the Labours of Hercules.

However, despite its popularity, the self-help industry is fraught with problems, not least of which is its reductionist approach to psychological and social issues. The genre often offers overly simplistic solutions to problems deeply rooted in systemic inequalities and socio-economic factors. For example, there is an emphasis on positive thinking, popularised by some book on the genre that suggests that individuals can manifest their desires simply through the power of thought. Still, this perspective disregards many systemic barriers, such as poverty, discrimination, climate change, wars, and lack of access to education and healthcare. By focusing on individual agency, the self-help literature often shifts the burden of change onto the individual, implicitly blaming them for their circumstances while ignoring the broader socio-political context.

The self-help industry frequently perpetuates a narrow definition of success, equating it with wealth, status and brands normally associated with physical appearance. This reinforces harmful societal norms and perpetuates feelings of inadequacy among those who do not conform to these ideals (McGee, 2005). The emphasis on personal responsibility and self-improvement can lead to victim blaming, where individuals who fail to succeed are seen as lacking the necessary willpower or discipline. This can be particularly damaging for vulnerable populations, who may already be struggling with issues such as low self-esteem, mental health problems, and socio-economic disadvantage. The commodification of self-help raises ethical concerns about the motives of those who profit from the industry. The proliferation of self-help books, seminars, coaches, gurus, mavericks of the human condition and online courses has created a lucrative market where success is often measured by book sales and social media followers rather than the actual impact on individuals' lives and communities. This commercialisation can lead to a dilution of meaningful content and critical analysis of one's life, as authors and "gurus" churn out generic advice to capitalise on trends rather than addressing the unique needs of their audience.

As this book will explore, the focus on individualism diverts attention away from collective struggles for social justice. Instead of challenging the systemic forces perpetuating inequality, self-help books encourage people to look inward and see their problems as personal failings rather than symptoms of more significant societal issues. The belief that anyone can succeed if they work hard enough is deeply flawed because it overlooks the significant structural barriers. By promoting the idea that success is entirely within one's control, self-help books obscure the realities of social and economic inequality. If people believe that their failure to succeed is due to a lack of effort or the wrong mindset, they are less likely to question the system's fairness. This, in turn, benefits those already in positions of power and wealth, as it reduces the likelihood of collective action or demands for redistribution. Even the most intimate aspects of our lives – emotions, self-esteem, and personal development – are marketed and sold as products. This commodification of personal growth exploits individuals' insecurities and reinforces consumerist values. These self-help books can distract people from the broader political and social issues that shape their lives by focusing on personal development and self-fulfilment. They can soothe and distract the public, preventing them from engaging in meaningful political action. This distraction is an inward focus that encourages people to solve their problems through personal change rather than collective action.

## Unpacking the Self-Help Paradox

Given the widespread influence of the self-help industry, a critical exploration is necessary to unpack the Self-Help Paradox – the gap between the promises of empowerment and the reality of superficial solutions. This involves questioning the assumptions that underpin self-help literature and discourse, such as the notion that personal success is solely a matter of individual effort. It also requires a deeper analysis of the socio-cultural factors that drive the demand for self-help, including the pressures of living in a neoliberal society that prioritises individualism and self-sufficiency. One criticism of the self-help industry is its failure to acknowledge the role of structural factors in shaping individuals' lives. By focusing on personal development and individual agency, self-help literature often overlooks how social, economic, and political forces constrain people's choices and opportunities. This can lead to "responsibilisation", where individuals are expected to manage their problems, even those resulting from systemic issues beyond their control (Rimke, 2000). Therefore, a critical examination of self-help involves challenging the narrative that success is solely a matter of personal effort and instead recognising the interplay between individual agency and social factors.

Self-help has become a multi-billion-dollar industry, raising questions about the motivations of those who produce and promote self-help products. Are they genuinely interested in helping people, or are they more concerned with profit-making? They might be genuinely interested in helping people. However, the commercialisation of self-help can also lead to a "one-size-fits-all" approach, where generic advice is sold to a mass audience without consideration for their context. This can result in a superficial and potentially harmful approach to personal development, where people are encouraged to adopt strategies that may not be appropriate for their particular circumstances.

In addition, questioning the assumptions and ethics of the self-help industry involves exploring the psychological and emotional impact of self-help literature on its consumers. While self-help books often promise to boost self-esteem and promote positive thinking, evidence suggests they can have the opposite effect. For example, research has shown that reading self-help books can lead to increased anxiety and depression, particularly when readers are unable to achieve the goals set out in the books (Gauntlett, 2008). Raymond et al. (2016) suggest that reading self-help books will probably not leave you feeling much better. Consumers of self-help books are more sensitive to stress and display more depressive symptoms than those who do not read such literature. This is because self-help literature often sets unrealistic expectations, making readers feel inadequate when they cannot live up to these ideals. Therefore, a critical examination of self-help involves questioning the psychological impact of these books and considering whether they are incredibly helpful or contribute to the very problems they claim to solve.

Self-help literature often relies on formulaic narratives that follow predictable patterns, making them accessible and appealing to a broad audience. One typical structure is "The hero's journey", where an individual begins in a state of struggle or dissatisfaction, embarks on a journey of self-discovery, faces various challenges, and achieves success or personal growth. This narrative is echoed in many self-help books, reinforcing the idea that everyone can be the hero of their own story if they follow the right steps. Another famous formula is "The turning point", in which a person hits rock bottom or encounters a significant life challenge that catalyses transformative change. This narrative resonates because it offers hope that even the lowest moments can lead to a brighter future. The transformation through habit formula is another common theme, suggesting that a person can gradually transform their life by changing small, daily habits. This approach emphasises the power of consistency and discipline in achieving long-term goals. The overcoming fear narrative focuses on confronting and overcoming deep-seated fears or limiting beliefs, leading to personal freedom or success. This storyline appeals to readers seeking to break free from self-imposed limitations. The power of positive thinking formula advocates a shift from negative to positive thinking, promising improved outcomes in various aspects of life. This concept, popularised by figures like Norman Vincent Peale, suggests that mindset is crucial to success. Finally, the success formula narrative revolves around discovering and consistently applying principles or strategies that lead to success. This formulaic approach implies that success can be achieved by anyone who adheres to a proven method. While varied in content, these narratives share a standard structure that simplifies complex human experiences into digestible, repeatable formulas.

The self-help industry promises a personal transformation in conveniently packaged paperbacks and overpriced seminars. It promotes the idea that we can overcome every hurdle life throws our way with a sprinkle of positive thinking, a dash of self-discipline, and perhaps an expensive course thrown in for good measure. However, beneath the glossy covers and affirming taglines lies a troubling ideology rooted in neoliberal individualism and psychological reductionism. The industry assumes that individuals are solely responsible for their circumstances. This belief, often summarised as "manifest your destiny" or "take control of your life", overlooks the structural inequalities and social determinants that shape people's lives. Poverty, racism, and sexism are not inconveniences to be overcome with positive thinking; they are deeply entrenched systems of power that require collective, systemic change. Yet, self-help books seldom address these forces, focusing instead on internal transformation as if fixing your mindset will magically dismantle these oppressive structures. The result is a narrative of blame: if you're struggling, it must be because you're not trying hard enough or haven't yet "unlocked" your potential. The self-help industry can exploit the genuine pain and suffering experienced by many people. In a world increasingly driven by precarious labour, economic instability, and rising mental health issues, it's little wonder people turn to self-help for solace. But instead of offering meaningful, community-driven solutions, it provides a series of simplistic, quick fixes that are doomed to fail. This failure, however, is often internalised by the individual, reinforcing the idea that they are the problem. The cycle of self-blame continues, with the self-help industry always on hand to sell the next fix – an endless loop of self-improvement capitalism. The self-help industry also commits a grave disservice by reducing the complexity of human experience to a set of generalised, often vacuous, platitudes. Books like *The Secret* promote the "law of attraction", suggesting that positive thoughts can attract success and wealth, an oversimplification of human psychology that borders magical thinking. This reductionist approach ignores the vast body of psychological research that highlights the role of social context, relational dynamics, and emotional complexity in shaping human behaviour. People are not isolated agents floating in a vacuum, yet the self-help narrative encourages us to see ourselves as such, perpetuating a myopic view of personal development.

The purpose of this book is not to dismiss the value of self-help literature outright but to provide a critical perspective that encourages readers to reflect on the content they consume. This involves highlighting the potential benefits of self-help, such as how it can empower individuals to take control of their lives, while also pointing out its limitations and the dangers of relying too heavily on self-help solutions. The tone of this book, in critiquing the self-help industry, is informed by scepticism, inviting readers to question the assumptions that underpin self-help literature and to consider the broader social, economic, and political factors that influence our lives. At the same time, this book aims to avoid being overly dismissive, recognising that many people find genuine value in self-help and that it can play a role in personal development. The self-help industry represents the phenomenon of human experience as having straightforward solutions and that warrants a critical examination. While self-help literature can offer valuable tools for personal growth, it also has significant limitations. It can contribute to perpetuating harmful societal norms and individual feelings of inadequacy or, as a good friend said: "F*** the self-help industry!"

# Chapter 1

# The Evolution of the Self-Help Industry

The self-help industry, a multi-billion-pound enterprise, traces its roots back much further than most of us realise. While the contemporary landscape of self-help is dominated by glossy paperbacks, motivational seminars, and influencer-led wellness movements, its origins are deeply embedded in the cultural and intellectual currents of the nineteenth century. Understanding the history and evolution of the self-help industry is essential to critically appraising its current manifestation, particularly given its profound influence on modern society's understanding of personal agency, success, and well-being. In its earliest form, the self-help genre can be traced to the moral and religious tracts of the nineteenth century. During this period, the emphasis on personal responsibility and self-improvement reflected broader societal changes brought about by the Industrial Revolution and the rise of the middle class. One of the seminal works that laid the groundwork for the self-help genre was Samuel Smiles's *Self-Help*, published in 1866. Smiles's book, which extolled the virtues of hard work, perseverance, and frugality, was not merely a guide for personal improvement but also a manifesto of Victorian values (Smiles, 1866). His assertion that "Heaven helps those who help themselves" encapsulated the spirit of the age, where individual success was seen as both a moral duty and a social imperative.

Smiles's work, however, was more than just a product of its time; it marked a shift towards a secular form of self-improvement that would become the cornerstone of the modern self-help movement. Before this, guidance on personal conduct and improvement was primarily dispensed through religious teachings. The shift towards a secularised, individual-centred approach to personal development reflected the broader secularisation of society and the increasing importance placed on individualism (Rimke, 2000). This laid the foundation for the self-help industry as we know it today, where the focus is squarely on the individual's capacity to shape their destiny, independent of religious or communal frameworks.

## From Positive Thinking to Self-Actualisation to Social Media

The early twentieth century saw the self-help genre evolve in response to new psychological theories and the changing socio-economic landscape. One of the most significant developments during this period was the rise of the positive thinking movement, epitomised by works such as *The Power of Positive Thinking* by Norman Vincent Peale (2012). Peale's book, which combined Christian ethics with psychological techniques to promote optimism and self-confidence, became a bestseller and laid the groundwork for the proliferation of self-help books that promised material success and personal happiness. Positive thinking, as a concept, was deeply intertwined with the American Dream – the idea that anyone, regardless of their background, could achieve success through hard work and a positive attitude (Illouz, 2008). This was particularly appealing in post-war America, where the self-help genre found fertile ground among a population eager for stability and prosperity. However, the emphasis on positive thinking also marked a significant shift in the self-help narrative – from focusing on moral and ethical self-improvement to a more individualistic pursuit of happiness and success.

By the mid-twentieth century, the influence of humanistic psychology, particularly the work of Abraham Maslow, had further shaped the self-help industry. For example, Maslow's hierarchy of needs and the concept of self-actualisation – where individuals strive to realise their full potential – resonated with the growing emphasis on personal fulfilment (Maslow, 1943). Maslow's hierarchy of needs is one of the most well-known theories in psychology, often depicted as a pyramid with basic physiological needs at the base, ascending through safety, love/belonging and esteem, and culminating in self-actualisation at the apex (Maslow, 1943). While it has undoubtedly influenced fields ranging from psychology to business and self-help, Maslow's model has significant limitations. These criticisms challenge its universality and cultural bias, and the linear progression it suggests. Maslow's hierarchy assumes a rigid, linear progression of needs. According to Maslow, individuals must satisfy lower-level needs (e.g., physiological and safety) before progressing to higher-level needs like self-actualisation. However, empirical evidence suggests that this hierarchy is not as fixed as Maslow proposed. For example, research by Wahba and Bridwell (1976) found little empirical support for the idea that needs are organised in a strict hierarchy. People often pursue higher-level needs even when lower-level needs are not fully met. Consider individuals in war-torn regions or those living in poverty who still seek meaning, connection, and self-fulfilment despite ongoing threats to their basic survival. This challenges the notion that human motivation can be neatly compartmentalised and suggests that needs might be more fluid and context-dependent than Maslow's model allows.

Maslow's hierarchy has been criticised for its cultural bias, particularly its emphasis on individualistic values. Self-actualisation – an idea rooted in individual achievement and personal growth – may resonate with some cultures prioritising autonomy and self-expression. However, it may not hold the same significance in collectivist cultures, where community, family, and social cohesion are often valued above individual aspirations. Researchers such as Hofstede (1984) have pointed out that in many non-Western cultures, the fulfilment of social or collective needs may take precedence over individual self-actualisation, which challenges the universality of Maslow's hierarchy. Another flaw in Maslow's model is that it is vague and difficult to operationalise. Maslow admitted that self-actualisation is rare, characterised by vague attributes such as creativity, spontaneity, and problem-solving (Maslow, 1970). The subjective nature of these qualities makes them challenging to measure or apply universally, raising questions about the practicality of striving for such an elusive goal. Self-actualisation is more of a philosophical ideal than a tangible psychological state.

This era saw the self-help genre expand beyond simple formulae for success to encompass a broader psychological and emotional well-being range. The idea that individuals could achieve not just success but also a deeper sense of self-fulfilment became a central tenet of the self-help industry, one that continues to dominate the genre today. The latter half of the twentieth century saw the self-help industry undergo significant commodification. The genre expanded beyond books to include seminars, workshops, and other products designed to capitalise on the burgeoning demand for personal development. This period also witnessed the rise of the self-help "guru" – charismatic figures who built empires around their brand and philosophy. Figures like Robbins, whose fire-walking seminars and motivational speaking engagements became synonymous with the self-help movement, exemplified this trend (McGee, 2005). Robbins and others like him turned self-help into big business, with the focus increasingly shifting towards the commercialisation of self-improvement. The commodification of self-help during this period also reflected broader societal trends, including the rise of consumer culture and the increasing emphasis on individualism. With its promise of personal transformation, the self-help industry tapped into the anxieties and aspirations of a generation grappling with rapid social and economic change. However, this also led to a dilution of the genre, with self-help becoming increasingly formulaic and superficial. The emphasis on quick fixes and easy solutions often came at the expense of deeper, more meaningful engagement with the issues (Starker, 2002).

The turn of the twenty-first century brought new challenges and opportunities for the self-help industry. The rise of the internet and social media platforms transformed how self-help content was produced and consumed. Online courses, blogs, podcasts, and social media influencers became new channels for dispensing self-help advice, often focusing on wellness and holistic health. The wellness movement, which encompasses everything from mindfulness and yoga to clean eating and alternative medicine, has become one of the dominant trends within the self-help industry in recent years (Illouz, 2008). The wellness trend represents a shift from the traditional self-help focus on financial success and career advancement to a more holistic well-being approach. This reflects broader societal changes, including growing concerns about mental health, stress, and work-life balance. However, the wellness movement is not without its critics. The commodification of wellness has led to concerns about its accessibility and the perpetuation of unrealistic ideals, particularly on social media platforms where the pressure to present a curated, "perfect" life can be overwhelming (Ehrenreich, 2009). Moreover, the wellness industry, like the broader self-help industry, often places the onus on the individual to manage their well-being while ignoring the structural and systemic factors that contribute to issues such as stress and anxiety.

## The Billion-Dollar Business of Self-Help

What began as a niche market in the mid-twentieth century has since ballooned into a sprawling enterprise encompassing books, seminars, online courses, apps, and celebrity-endorsed wellness products. The industry's evolution from the modest beginnings of motivational literature to a commodified enterprise is a testament to its extraordinary ability to adapt to changing cultural currents and the relentless pursuit of self-optimisation that characterises contemporary society.

At its core, the self-help industry thrives on the perpetual promise of personal transformation. From achieving financial success to improving relationships and enhancing mental well-being, self-help products cater to various human desires. The charm of self-help is rooted in its simple, often formulaic, prescriptions for complex life issues, offering a roadmap to success that appears to be within anyone's reach. This appeal has enabled the industry to penetrate diverse demographics, making it both culturally pervasive and economically formidable. This growth is fuelled by a combination of factors, including the increasing mainstream awareness of mental health and wellness issues, the rise of digital platforms that democratise access to self-help resources, and the relentless marketing strategies that tap into consumers' insecurities and aspirations. In the United States alone, self-improvement market books remain a cornerstone of the self-help industry, generating significant revenue for publishers. The genre consistently ranks among the top-performing categories in the publishing world. In 2020 alone, self-help books generated over $800 million in revenue in the United States, making it one of the most profitable segments in the book industry (Anderson, 2022). This success is not confined to traditional print; the digitalisation of self-help content has also spurred growth in audiobook and e-book formats, catering to an increasingly tech-savvy audience.

Beyond books, the self-help industry has diversified into many other products and services. Motivational speaking and personal coaching have emerged as highly profitable avenues, with some figures commanding fees upwards of $300,000 per speaking engagement. Often styled as transformative experiences, these events draw thousands of participants willing to pay premium prices for the promise of life-changing insights. The seminar business alone is estimated to be worth around $500 million annually in the United States (Marketdata LLC, 2020). It is noted as the $11 billion personal development industry. The digital revolution has further amplified the reach and profitability of the self-help industry. Online courses, webinars, and coaching services have become increasingly popular, driven by platforms. These platforms offer a wide range of self-improvement courses, from mindfulness meditation to entrepreneurial skills, often at a fraction of the cost of traditional education. The global e-learning market, which includes self-help courses, was valued at $250 billion in 2020 and is expected to grow to $1 trillion by 2027 (Global Market Insights, 2021). This surge reflects not only the growing demand for accessible personal development resources but also the increasing acceptance of digital learning as a legitimate and valuable form of education.

Moreover, the rise of social media and influencer culture has profoundly impacted the self-help industry. Influencers, many of whom lack formal qualifications, have become the new personal development gurus, leveraging their platforms to promote self-help products and services. This phenomenon has led to the proliferation of wellness products, ranging from dietary supplements to mindfulness apps, often marketed to achieve a better, more fulfilled life. The wellness industry, which overlaps with self-help, is another colossal market, which was valued at $4.4 trillion globally in 2020 (Global Wellness Institute, 2021). This convergence of self-help and wellness reflects a broader trend in consumer culture, where health, beauty, and personal success are increasingly commodified and sold as interconnected goals.

Despite its undeniable financial success, the efficacy of self-help products must be questioned. While some individuals may benefit from the advice and strategies offered, a growing body of research suggests that self-help interventions are often no more effective than a placebo and, in some cases, may even be harmful (Rosen, Glasgow, & Moore, 1993). The pressure to achieve the idealised outcomes promised by self-help can lead to feelings of failure and inadequacy, exacerbating rather than alleviating psychological distress. The lack of regulation in the industry means that consumers are often exposed to pseudoscientific or misleading claims, particularly in areas such as health and wellness. The commercialisation of self-help also raises ethical concerns. The industry's reliance on marketing strategies that exploit consumers' insecurities and desire for quick fixes can be seen as manipulative and predatory. This is particularly evident in the proliferation of "get rich quick" schemes and "miracle cures" that promise instant results with little effort. These products often prey on vulnerable individuals, offering false hope and diverting attention from more effective, evidence-based interventions. The ethical implications of profiting from such practices are significant and warrant greater scrutiny from regulators and consumers. The self-help industry, a sprawling domain where the personal and the profitable intersect, owes much of its growth and influence to a select group of key figures and the seminal books they authored. These writers have shaped the contours of the self-help genre and left indelible marks on popular culture and individual psyches.

As mentioned previously, we cannot discuss the self-help genre without mentioning Samuel Smiles, widely regarded as the father of self-help literature. His 1859 book, *Self-Help*, is often credited with initiating the genre and laying the groundwork for its development. Smiles's book, which emphasised self-reliance, perseverance, and moral integrity, was a product of the Victorian ethos, reflecting the values of hard work and personal responsibility, which were central to the era's social and economic life (Smiles, 1859). Broadly, Victorian worldviews refer to the set of moral values and social attitudes that characterised the Victorian era, spanning Queen Victoria's reign from 1837 to 1901. At its core, this worldview emphasised hard work, self-discipline, and personal responsibility as pathways to individual and societal success. It was deeply rooted in the belief that moral integrity and perseverance were essential for social mobility and the betterment of society. A strong sense of duty also underpinned the Victorian spirit of oneself, and others reflected in the era's emphasis on charity, temperance, and adherence to social norms. This moral framework was heavily influenced by Christian values, particularly those related to thrift, modesty, and the sanctity of the family unit. The period was marked by a clear division between the deserving and undeserving poor, with the former viewed as individuals who could uplift themselves through effort and virtue and the latter often seen as morally deficient. The Victorians promoted a worldview where success was attainable through moral virtue and persistent effort, while failure was usually attributed to personal shortcomings rather than structural factors. These views profoundly shaped the social and cultural aspects of the time and left a legacy that is very much linked to Western notions of morality and success.

While today's standards somewhat date Smiles's work, his influence cannot be overstated. It set the tone for subsequent self-help literature, which often echoes his emphasis on individual effort and moral character. Fast forward to the twentieth century, and the figure of Dale Carnegie looms large. Carnegie's 1936 book, *How to Win Friends and Influence People*, remains one of the best-selling self-help books ever. Carnegie's work capitalised on the burgeoning corporate culture of the early twentieth century, offering readers practical advice on navigating social and professional relationships. The book's focus on interpersonal skills and emotional intelligence resonated with readers at a time when success increasingly depended on one's ability to network and build relationships (Carnegie, 1936). The title suggests an element of strategic influence – Carnegie's work has been instrumental in shaping the self-help genre's focus on communication and social skills. *The Power of Positive Thinking*, published in 1952, represents another significant milestone in the self-help genre. Peale, a Christian minister, combined religious faith with the principles of positive psychology to create a message that was both spiritually uplifting and applicable. His book, which advocates for the power of optimism and belief in oneself, struck a chord with readers in post-war America when the nation grappled with the challenges of the Cold War and the promises of economic prosperity. Peale's work is often critiqued for its overly simplistic view of human psychology, reducing emotional and mental health issues to mere deficits in positive thinking. Nevertheless, *The Power of Positive Thinking* has had a lasting impact, influenced countless other self-help authors and established positive thinking as a central theme.

*The 7 Habits of Highly Effective People* was published in 1989. Covey's book represents a synthesis of earlier self-help principles, combining personal responsibility, moral character, and positive thinking with a more structured approach to personal development. The book's appeal lies in its practical, habit-based framework, which offers readers a clear, step-by-step guide to success in both personal and professional life. Covey's emphasis on aligning one's actions with individual values and principles reflects a more holistic approach to self-help, acknowledging the importance of integrity and purpose alongside achievement. The enduring popularity of the *7 Habits* speaks to its effectiveness as a self-help tool and it remains a staple in the genre. Tony Robbins is another influential figure in the self-help industry, whose bombastic personality and larger-than-life presence have made him a household name. Robbins's 1991 book, *Awaken the Giant Within*, encapsulates his self-help approach, which focuses on empowerment, self-mastery, and massive action to achieve one's goals. Robbins's style is notably different from his predecessors', incorporating elements of motivational speaking, neuro-linguistic programming (NLP), and high-energy seminars that promise to deliver life-changing results. While critics often point to the lack of empirical evidence supporting many of Robbins's techniques, his impact on the self-help industry is undeniable. His ability to inspire and mobilise large audiences has helped popularise the idea that personal development is not just a solitary pursuit but one that can be energised through shared experience. The influence of Rhonda Byrne's *The Secret*, published in 2006, highlights the ongoing evolution of the self-help genre in the twenty-first century. Byrne's book, which popularised the concept of the law of attraction, suggests that positive or negative thoughts can directly influence one's life circumstances. *The Secret* was a cultural phenomenon, due to its media exposure and the endorsement of high-profile personalities. However, the book has been widely criticised for promoting a pseudoscientific view of reality, where thinking positively is framed as a panacea for all life's challenges. Despite these criticisms, *The Secret* has significantly impacted contemporary self-help culture, particularly its emphasis on manifestation and the power of the mind. This theme continues to resonate with audiences today.

It is also worth mentioning the contributions of figures like Louise Hay and Deepak Chopra, who have brought a more holistic, spiritually oriented approach to self-help. Hay's 1984 book, *You Can Heal Your Life*, posits that mental and physical health are deeply interconnected and that positive affirmations can heal both the body and the mind (Hay, 1984). Chopra has blended Eastern spiritual traditions with Western self-help principles in books like *The Seven Spiritual Laws of Success* (1994), promoting a more integrative approach to personal development that includes meditation, mindfulness, and spiritual growth (Chopra, 1994). These authors have expanded the scope of self-help to include not just the mind and behaviour but also the body and spirit, reflecting a broader cultural shift towards holistic wellness. While these figures and books have been instrumental in shaping the self-help industry, the success of these self-help icons is often tied to their ability to tap into societal anxieties and aspirations, offering simple solutions to such problems. The self-help industry is as much about selling hope as it is about personal growth. The commodification of self-help has led to a proliferation of content that often prioritises marketability over substance. Books and programmes are frequently packaged with catchy titles and easy-to-follow steps. Still, they may lack the depth, ethics and scientific rigour necessary to address the underlying issues they purport to solve.

## Marketing and Selling Hope

The self-help industry, a multi-billion-dollar global enterprise, has become pervasive in contemporary culture, shaping how individuals perceive and pursue personal development. At its core, the industry operates on a simple yet powerful promise: that anyone, regardless of their circumstances, can achieve happiness, success, and fulfilment by applying certain principles or techniques. As a critical observer, one must question how this industry effectively markets and sells this promise of hope, often blurring the lines between genuine empowerment and the commodification of psychological well-being. The self-help industry thrives on commodifying hope and packaging it as a product that can be bought, sold, and consumed. This commodification is evident in the vast array of books, seminars, workshops, online courses, and motivational speeches that flood the market. Each product offers a unique pathway to a better life, often framed in terms of quickly digestible steps or formulae. For instance, popular titles (Sincero, 2013) promise readers the keys to unlocking their potential and manifesting their desires through positive thinking and self-belief. However, this commodification raises essential questions about the nature of the hope being sold. The industry often promotes an oversimplified and individualistic view of personal development, suggesting that success and happiness are solely within the individual's control. This perspective neglects the web of socio-economic factors that may be involved.

The marketing strategies employed by the self-help industry are meticulously designed to tap into the deep-seated human desire for hope and transformation. These strategies often involve the use of emotionally charged language, compelling narratives, and the promise of quick, easy solutions to life's challenges. For example, the ubiquitous phrases "You can do it!" or "You got this!" serve as both a rallying cry and a marketing slogan, encouraging consumers to believe they can overcome any obstacle with the right mindset. Self-help authors and gurus frequently present themselves as living testimonials to the efficacy of their methods, sharing personal stories of triumph over adversity. This narrative approach humanises the author and creates a parasocial relationship with the reader, fostering a sense of trust and credibility (Cohen, 2004). The reader is led to believe that if the author could succeed, they too can do the same, provided they follow the prescribed steps. The self-help industry often employs the "success story" concept as a powerful marketing tool. Success stories, whether real or fabricated, are used to create a sense of possibility and to reinforce the idea that transformation is within reach. As McGee (2005) notes, these stories are strategically crafted to evoke hope, presenting a simplified reality where perseverance and positivity inevitably lead to success. The underlying message is clear: failure is not an option, and those who fail have only themselves to blame.

At the heart of the self-help industry's appeal is its ability to tap into the psychology of hope. As a psychological construct, hope is a powerful motivator that can inspire individuals to set and pursue goals, even in the face of adversity (Snyder, 2002).

The self-help industry capitalises on this by framing hope as both the means and the end of personal development. In other words, self-help products sell the promise of hope and position it as the key to unlocking one's potential. The commercialisation of hope within the self-help industry raises ethical concerns. The constant emphasis on positive thinking and self-empowerment can lead to what Ehrenreich (2009) terms "toxic positivity", where individuals are encouraged to suppress negative emotions and ignore the realities of their circumstances in favour of an artificially optimistic outlook. This can be particularly harmful for individuals facing significant life challenges, as it may lead them to internalise their struggles as personal failures rather than recognise the broader systemic issues at play. A typical example of toxic positivity found in many self-help books is the phrase "Just stay positive, and everything will work out". While well-intentioned, this advice can be harmful because it oversimplifies complex situations and emotions, implying that negative feelings or challenges can be overcome by maintaining a positive attitude. This type of advice often ignores the genuine and valid emotions people experience during difficult times, such as grief, anxiety, or frustration. It suggests that if someone is struggling, it's because they aren't being positive enough, which can lead to feelings of guilt or inadequacy. This form of toxic positivity dismisses the need to process negative emotions, seek support, or address the underlying issues, instead promoting a superficial sense of optimism that can be both invalidating and unhelpful. The self-help industry's focus on hope as a product can create a cycle of dependency, where consumers continually seek out new books, seminars, and courses in the quest for self-improvement. Each new product promises to be the definitive solution, yet often leaves the consumer feeling unfulfilled, leading them to purchase the next offering in the hope that it will finally provide the answers they seek (Illouz, 2008). This cycle perpetuates the industry's profitability and reinforces the idea that personal growth is an endless journey that requires constant investment.

The self-help industry's marketing and sale of hope raises significant ethical questions about the responsibilities of those who profit from it. While there is no denying that some self-help products have the potential to inspire and empower individuals, there is a fine line between genuine support and exploitation. As Furedi (2004) argues, the industry often preys on the vulnerabilities of its audience, offering false hope in exchange for financial gain. This is particularly concerning given the lack of regulation in the self-help industry, which allows for the proliferation of dubious claims and pseudoscientific practices. The ethical concerns are further compounded by the fact that the self-help industry often targets individuals who are already marginalised or struggling with mental health issues. The promise of hope and transformation can be incredibly alluring to those who feel lost, isolated, or powerless, making them prime targets for marketing strategies that exploit their desire for change. In this context, the self-help industry can be seen as both a symptom and a driver of a culture that puts undue pressure on individuals to "fix" themselves rather than addressing the broader social and economic factors contributing to their struggles.

The self-help industry's focus on individualism and personal responsibility can be seen as antithetical to collective empowerment and social justice principles. Addressing systemic issues and assisting environments that promote well-being for all members of society is important rather than requiring individuals to overcome their challenges in isolation. The self-help industry's marketing of hope can be critiqued for its failure to acknowledge the role of community, support networks, and social structures in shaping individual outcomes. While self-help products may offer valuable tools for personal growth, they are not a substitute for the collective action and systemic change needed to address the root causes of social and psychological distress.

The self-help industry, as we know it today, is a product of centuries of cultural, intellectual, and social evolution. What began in the nineteenth century as a genre deeply rooted in moral and religious teachings has transformed into a multi-billion-pound enterprise, reflecting and shaping modern society's values, aspirations, and anxieties. The journey from Samuel Smiles's *Self-Help* to the contemporary wellness movement reveals the industry's adaptability and its deep entanglement with the socio-economic and cultural shifts that have occurred over the past two centuries. Smiles's work, which laid the foundation for the self-help genre, was more than just a reflection of Victorian values; it marked the beginning of a secular approach to personal development that prioritised individual effort over collective or religious salvation. This shift was emblematic of broader societal changes, as the rise of the middle class and the Industrial Revolution redefined success and personal responsibility. The evolution continued through the twentieth century, with the advent of positive thinking and humanistic psychology, which further emphasised the individual's capacity for self-actualisation and personal fulfilment. Figures like Norman Vincent Peale and Abraham Maslow introduced concepts central to the genre – optimism, self-confidence, and pursuing one's true potential. As the industry grew, so did its scope and influence. The commodification of self-help in the latter half of the twentieth century saw the rise of charismatic gurus and the proliferation of seminars, workshops, and, eventually, digital content. This period was characterised by the industry's increasing focus on quick fixes and easy solutions, often at the expense of more profound, more meaningful engagement with the complexities of personal development. The rise of the wellness movement in the twenty-first century further expanded the industry's reach, blending self-help with holistic health and lifestyle practices. The industry's emphasis on individualism and personal responsibility often overlooks the social, cultural, and economic factors that shape individual lives. As the self-help genre has grown into a commercial drive, it has sometimes prioritised profit over substance. The challenge moving forward is to critically engage with the self-help industry, recognising its potential for empowerment while remaining aware of its limitations and the broader societal implications of its message. The history of self-help is a testament to its enduring appeal, but it also serves as a reminder that personal growth cannot be disentangled from the context in which it occurs.

# Chapter 2

# The Problem with Self-Help: Oversimplification and Individualism

"The human condition" is often thrown around in philosophical debates, literature, and casual conversations. But what does it mean? At its core, the human condition refers to the various elements of human existence – the joys, the sorrows, the struggles, and the triumphs that make up our lives. It's the experience of being alive, of navigating a beautiful and terrifying world full of potential yet fraught with limitations. But here is the thing: understanding the human condition is far from straightforward. Why is it so complex? Humans are not simple creatures. We are beings of contradictions. We crave connection, yet we often find ourselves feeling alone. We seek happiness but sometimes we sabotage our own chances of finding it. We have an incredible capacity for love, compassion, creativity, hate, cruelty, and destruction. We are, in many ways, a mystery even to ourselves. One of the most perplexing aspects of the human condition is our emotions. Emotions are powerful, driving much of what we do, yet they are often unpredictable and contradictory. We can simultaneously feel joy and sadness or love someone while resenting them. Our emotions can guide us to make wise decisions, but they can also lead us astray, clouding our judgement and making us act against our own best interests. Trying to make sense of our emotions is like trying to catch the wind – they are intangible and ever-changing.

You can feel it brush against your skin, stir the leaves, and hear it whistle through the trees, but the moment you try to grasp it, it slips through your fingers. Just like the wind, our lives are all invisible, yet undeniably natural forces – emotions, thoughts, desires, and fears – are all swirling around us, shaping our existence in subtle and profound ways. We chase after happiness, love, meaning, and success, believing that if we reach out far enough, we can hold onto them. But, like the wind, we cannot capture and keep these aspects of life. They are fluid, ever-changing, and often beyond our control. One moment, we might feel the exhilaration of the wind at our backs, propelling us forward with joy and purpose. The next, we are buffeted by storms of doubt, grief, and uncertainty, struggling to stay upright. Yet, just as the wind cannot be captured, it can be harnessed. Sailors have long known how to use the wind's power to navigate vast oceans, adjusting their sails to work with the forces of nature rather than against them. We may never be able to hold onto the wind – or the elusive certainties we seek. In embracing the unpredictability and transience of life, we discover the true art of living – not in capturing the wind.

Then there is the issue of identity. Who are we? Is our identity something fixed, or is it constantly evolving? We often define ourselves by our roles – student, parent, worker, friend – but these roles can change, leaving us to question who we are without them. Our sense of self is shaped by our experiences, our relationships, and the society we live in. Still, it is also something deeply personal that can't be fully understood or explained by anyone else. Let us not forget the existential questions that have plagued humanity for centuries. Why are we here? What is the purpose of life? Is there a meaning to all of this, or are we just specks in an indifferent universe? These questions can be unsettling, but they are also a crucial part of what it means to be human. The search for meaning is a journey that each of us undertakes in our own way, and the answers – or lack thereof – can shape our lives. The human condition is not just a matter of individual experience. We are shaped by our communities, the social structures surrounding us, and the broader cultural narratives that inform our understanding of the world. Our struggles often reflect more extensive societal issues – inequality, injustice, and oppression – and addressing these requires more than individual effort; it requires collective action and systemic change. So, yes, the human condition is puzzling, full of contradictions and mysteries that we may never fully unravel. But it is also what makes life rich and meaningful. It's why we create art, write poetry, and tell stories. It's what drives us to connect with others, to seek out new experiences, and to ask the big questions. And while we may never find all the answers, the journey of exploring the human condition is a vital part of what it means to be alive.

In the vast, sprawling landscape of the self-help industry, one message rings out louder than all the rest: that there exists a single, universal formula for happiness, success, and personal fulfilment – a "one-size-fits-all" solution that can be applied to every person, regardless of their unique circumstances. It is an alluring proposition that promises simplicity and clarity in a world that often feels overwhelming and chaotic. This notion is not just misleading – it can be dangerous. The idea that one method, approach, or set of principles can be universally applied to solve the myriad challenges humans face is a fallacy, a convenient fiction that the self-help industry perpetuates to sell books, seminars, and online courses. It ignores the rich diversity of human experience. The problem with the "one-size-fits-all" approach is that it assumes all individuals are the same – that we all have the same needs and goals, and capacity to achieve them. This assumption is not only false but also reductive. Humans are not homogeneous; we are products of our environments, cultures, genetics, and personal histories. Each of us carries unique experiences, traumas, strengths, and weaknesses that shape who we are and how we navigate the world. To suggest that a single solution could be effective for everyone is to ignore the role of external forces entirely. It is akin to offering the same pair of shoes to every person, regardless of their size, and expecting them to fit perfectly.

The "one-size-fits-all" approach often fails to account for the social determinants of health and well-being – factors such as socio-economic status, education, race, and gender profoundly impact a person's ability to thrive. For example, a self-help book that preaches the power of positive thinking may resonate with someone with financial stability who wants to take risks and pursue their dreams. But for someone living in poverty, struggling to meet their basic needs, the idea that their situation can be improved simply by "thinking positively" is not just unrealistic – it is crude. It places the burden of change entirely on the individual without acknowledging the systemic barriers holding them back (Marmot, 2005).

This individualistic focus is a hallmark of the self-help industry and one of its most significant flaws. By promoting the idea that personal success is entirely within the individual's control, the industry effectively absolves society of any responsibility for addressing the structural inequalities that contribute to many of the problems people face. It reinforces the neoliberal narrative that individuals are solely responsible for their fate while ignoring the broader social, economic, and political forces that shape our lives (Giroux, 2008). This is not to say that personal responsibility is unimportant – taking charge of one's life is often a necessary step towards personal growth. But it is not sufficient on its own, and suggesting otherwise is perpetuating a dangerous myth. Another issue with the "one-size-fits-all" approach is that it often promotes a narrow definition of success, one that is rooted in material wealth, career achievement, and social status. This definition is not only limiting but also exclusionary, as it fails to recognise how people can lead fulfilling lives. For instance, a person who values family and community over career advancement may not find the advice in many self-help books relevant or helpful. Similarly, someone who measures success by their contributions to society rather than by the size of their bank account may find themselves alienated by a self-help industry that equates personal worth with financial success. This narrow focus on material success also perpetuates the idea that happiness can be bought and is something to be achieved rather than experienced. Happiness is an emotion that cannot be reduced to a simple formula or checklist (Diener & Seligman, 2004). The self-help industry's reliance on anecdotal evidence is another critical flaw in the "one-size-fits-all" approach. Many self-help books are written by individuals who have experienced personal success and believe their methods can be universally applied. However, these success stories are often highly contextual and may not be replicable in different circumstances. What worked for one person may not work for another, and the failure to acknowledge this fact can lead to frustration, disappointment, and a sense of inadequacy for those unable to achieve the same results. This reliance on anecdotal evidence also raises questions about the validity of the advice offered. Unlike evidence-based practices, which are grounded in scientific research and rigorously assessed, many self-help methods are based on their authors' personal experiences and opinions. While these experiences can be valuable, they do not constitute a universal truth and should not be presented as such (Lilienfeld, 2007).

The "one-size-fits-all" approach can be particularly harmful when applied to mental health. Mental health is deeply personal, and what works for one person may not work for another. For example, a self-help book that promotes mindfulness as a tool to manage anxiety may be beneficial for some. Still, it may not be effective for someone whose anxiety is rooted in trauma. Moreover, the promotion of self-help methods as a substitute for professional mental health care can be dangerous, as it may discourage individuals from seeking the help they need (Furedi, 2004). Mental health treatment should be tailored to individuals, considering their unique experiences, needs, and circumstances. The idea that a single method or technique can address all mental distress might not be helpful. In addition to the psychological and social implications, the "one-size-fits-all" approach raises ethical concerns. By promoting a universal solution, the self-help industry risks exploiting vulnerable individuals searching for answers and willing to pay for the promise of a better life. This exploitation is compounded by the fact that the industry is largely unregulated, allowing for the proliferation of dubious products and services that may not be effective or, in some cases, may even be harmful. This lack of regulation also means there is little accountability for the claims made by self-help authors and gurus, leaving people vulnerable to misinformation and false expectations (Illouz, 2008). The self-help industry's focus on quick fixes and instant gratification exacerbates the problem. In a world where people increasingly seek instant solutions and answers, the promise of a "one-size-fits-all" solution is particularly appealing. However, personal growth and development are not quick processes; they require time, effort, and often the support of others. The idea that lasting change can be achieved overnight by applying a simple formula is unrealistic and undermines the importance of perseverance, resilience, and community support in personal development (McGee, 2005). The "one-size-fits-all" approach fails to recognise the importance of cultural context in shaping human behaviour and well-being. What works in one culture may not work in another, and the imposition of Western self-help methods on individuals from different cultural backgrounds can be both ineffective and culturally insensitive. For example, a self-help book that promotes assertiveness as the key to success may resonate with individuals from individualistic cultures. Still, it may not be relevant or appropriate for those from collectivist cultures, where harmony and group cohesion are valued over individual assertiveness (Triandis, 1995). By ignoring the cultural dimensions of human experience, the self-help industry risks perpetuating a narrow and ethnocentric view of personal development.

## The Myth of Personal Responsibility
## for Systemic Problems

In the current context, where the self-help industry thrives and individualism is often celebrated as the pinnacle of success, personal responsibility has become a dominant narrative. This idea – that each individual is solely responsible for their successes and failures, and by extension, their happiness and misery – has permeated every aspect of our culture. It is propagated by self-help gurus, perpetuated by motivational speakers, and even enshrined in public policy. However, while alluring in its simplicity, this narrative can be flawed. It oversimplifies societal issues and places an undue burden on individuals to solve problems that are, in fact, systemic. This myth of personal responsibility obscures the reality that many of the challenges individuals face are not merely the result of personal failings but are deeply rooted in larger social, economic, and political structures that limit opportunities and perpetuate inequality. The concept of personal responsibility has been instrumentalised by neoliberal ideologies, which emphasise free markets, deregulation, and minimal government intervention. Neoliberalism posits that individuals are rational actors who make choices in a free market and that these choices determine their outcomes in life. According to this view, success results from hard work, perseverance, and intelligent decision-making, while failure is attributed to laziness, poor choices, or a lack of discipline. This framework conveniently ignores the structural factors that influence an individual's ability to succeed, such as access to quality education, healthcare, and economic opportunities. As Harvey (2005) notes, neoliberalism has reconfigured the concept of citizenship to emphasise self-reliance and individual responsibility, effectively shifting the burden of social problems from the state to the individual. The perniciousness of the personal responsibility narrative lies in its ability to shift blame away from systemic issues and onto individuals. For instance, consider the problem of poverty. In a society that subscribes to the myth of personal responsibility, poverty is often viewed as a personal failure. People experiencing poverty are blamed for their circumstances, poor financial decisions, not working hard or saving enough. This perspective is not only myopic but also profoundly unjust, as it ignores the structural causes of poverty, such as wage stagnation, lack of affordable housing, and the erosion of the social safety net. As Rank (2004) argues, poverty is primarily the result of structural factors rather than individual deficiencies. The belief that poverty is solely the fault of the individual serves to obscure these systemic issues and absolve society of the responsibility to address them.

The myth of personal responsibility also manifests in health and wellness. Individuals are bombarded with messages about the importance of healthy eating, regular exercise, and stress management as the keys to a long and healthy life. While these behaviours are undoubtedly important, the focus on individual health choices often ignores the social determinants of health – factors such as income, education, neighbourhood environment, and access to healthcare – that significantly impact health outcomes. For example, a person living in a low-income neighbourhood may have limited access to fresh produce, safe spaces for physical activity, and quality healthcare, making it much more challenging to maintain a healthy lifestyle. Yet, when this person develops a chronic illness, they are often blamed for their condition rather than the systemic factors that contributed to it. As Marmot (2005) points out, social inequalities largely drive health inequalities, and addressing these requires systemic change rather than simply encouraging individuals to make better choices.

Education is another area where the myth of personal responsibility is particularly salient. The notion that every student has an equal opportunity to succeed, provided they work hard and apply themselves, is a cornerstone of the *American Dream*. However, this idealised view of education ignores the vast disparities in educational resources, quality, and opportunities between different communities. Students from wealthy families often have access to well-funded schools, private tutors, and extracurricular activities. In contrast, students from low-income families may attend underfunded schools with fewer resources and opportunities. Despite these disparities, the narrative of personal responsibility persists, placing the blame for academic failure squarely on the shoulders of the student rather than on the inequities in the education system. As Kozol (1991) highlights, the education system in the United States is deeply unequal, and these inequalities significantly determine student outcomes. By focusing solely on individual effort, we ignore the structural barriers that prevent many students from reaching their full potential. The criminal justice system also perpetuates the myth of personal responsibility, particularly in its treatment of marginalised communities. The "tough on crime" policies that gained popularity in the late twentieth century are based on the belief that individuals are fully responsible for their actions and should be held accountable, often through harsh punishments. However, this perspective ignores the social and economic conditions that contribute to criminal behaviour, such as poverty, lack of education, and limited job opportunities. The over-representation of people of colour in the criminal justice system is a stark reminder of the systemic racism and inequality that underpins these policies. As Alexander (2010) argues, the criminal justice system in the United States functions as a system of racial control, disproportionately targeting and punishing people of colour while ignoring the systemic factors that contribute to crime.

The myth of personal responsibility is not limited to the United States; it is a global phenomenon that affects how we understand and address social problems. In the context of climate change, for example, individuals are often encouraged to reduce their carbon footprint by making environmentally friendly choices, such as driving less, recycling, and conserving energy. While these actions are essential, they are insufficient to address the scale of the problem. The focus on individual responsibility detracts from the need for systemic change, such as transitioning to renewable energy sources, regulating corporate polluters, and implementing environmental justice policies. As Klein (2014) argues, addressing climate change requires a fundamental shift in our economic and political systems rather than simply asking individuals to change their behaviour.

The emphasis on personal responsibility also has profound psychological effects, particularly on those who cannot overcome the systemic barriers they face. The belief that success is solely the result of individual effort can lead to guilt, shame, and inadequacy when individuals cannot achieve their goals. This is particularly true for those who face multiple forms of disadvantage, such as poverty, racism, and discrimination. The pressure to succeed in the face of these challenges can be overwhelming, leading to stress, anxiety, and depression. As Foucault (1977) argues, internalising power – where individuals believe they are solely responsible for their success or failure – can be a powerful form of social control, keeping people in line and preventing them from challenging the status quo.

The personal responsibility myth also reinforces existing power structures by diverting attention away from the need for collective action and systemic change. When individuals are told they are solely responsible for their fate, they are less likely to question the social, economic, and political systems shaping their lives. This narrative supports the interests of those in power who benefit from maintaining the status quo. By focusing on individual solutions to systemic problems, we ignore the need for collective action to address the root causes of inequality and injustice. As Freire (1970) notes, true liberation requires a collective effort to transform the structures of society that perpetuate oppression. The myth of personal responsibility is also deeply ingrained in public policy, particularly in welfare and social services. Neoliberal policies emphasising responsibility have led to the dismantling of social safety nets and privatisation of services, with devastating consequences for those who rely on these services. The narrative that individuals should be self-reliant and not depend on government assistance has been used to justify cuts to welfare programmes, healthcare, and education, leaving the most vulnerable members of society to fend for themselves. According to Fording and Schram (2011), these policies are rooted in racialised assumptions about who is deserving of support, and serve to reinforce social hierarchies and maintain control over the marginalised.

## Overlooking Social, Cultural, and Economic Factors

The industry appears benevolent—helping individuals navigate life's challenges, achieve their dreams, and overcome adversity. However, a closer examination reveals a glaring oversight: the industry's systematic disregard for the social, cultural, and economic factors that shape individual lives. This oversight is not merely an academic critique but a fundamental flaw that renders much of the self-help advice ineffective, particularly for those marginalised by systemic inequalities. The idea is that each person is the architect of their destiny, capable of overcoming any obstacle through sheer willpower, positive thinking, and self-discipline. This narrative assumes that personal success or failure is solely a matter of individual effort. It suggests that if you are not successful, if you are not happy, if you are not achieving your goals, then the fault lies with you. You must work harder, think more positively, or follow the latest five-step programme to unlock your potential. This perspective ignores the profound influence of social, cultural, and economic factors on individual lives. It overlooks the fact that not everyone starts from the same place, that the playing field is far from level, and that some face obstacles, not merely personal challenges but systemic barriers.

For instance, while a self-help book might suggest that financial success is a matter of developing the right mindset and habits, it fails to consider the impact of growing up in poverty, attending underfunded schools, or facing racial and gender discrimination in the workplace. These are not challenges that can be overcome by positive thinking alone; they are structural issues that require systemic solutions. The social context in which individuals live plays a critical role in shaping their opportunities and outcomes. Research has consistently shown that social determinants such as education, housing, employment, and access to healthcare are major predictors of health and well-being (Marmot & Wilkinson, 2006). Yet, the self-help industry often promotes the idea that individuals are entirely responsible for their health, wealth, and happiness, disregarding the broader social forces at play. For example, a book on weight loss might focus on diet and exercise, offering tips on how to stay motivated and resist temptation. However, it is unlikely to address the fact that many live in "food deserts", where fresh, healthy food is hard to find and expensive to buy. Nor is it likely to discuss the stress and time constraints faced by low-income individuals working multiple jobs, which can make regular exercise a near impossibility. By focusing solely on individual behaviour, the self-help industry ignores the social and economic conditions contributing to health disparities, perpetuating the false notion that health is simply a matter of personal choice.

Cultural factors are also conspicuously absent from much of the self-help discourse. The industry is heavily dominated by Western ideals and values, particularly self-reliance, autonomy, and individual achievement. This cultural bias is evident in the language and concepts used in self-help literature, which often emphasises personal empowerment, self-optimisation, and the pursuit of individual goals. However, these values are not universally shared. In many cultures, the well-being of the community or family takes precedence over personal success. Collectivist cultures, for example, emphasise interdependence, social harmony, and the importance of relationships. In these contexts, the advice offered by self-help books may be irrelevant and counterproductive, encouraging behaviours that are at odds with cultural norms and values (Triandis, 1995). The self-help industry's focus on individualism can exacerbate feelings of isolation and disconnection, particularly in cultures where community and social bonds are central to identity and well-being. By promoting the idea that individuals should prioritise their own needs and goals above those of others, the industry inadvertently undermines the social support networks that are crucial for coping with life's challenges. This is particularly problematic in the context of mental health, where strong social ties are a protective factor against depression and anxiety (Cohen, 2004).

Economic factors, too, are often overlooked in the self-help narrative. The industry frequently targets middle-class consumers with disposable income to purchase books, attend seminars, and invest in self-improvement programmes. These consumers are often better positioned to benefit from the advice offered, as they have the financial stability, education, and social capital to change their lives. However, the barriers to self-improvement are much higher for those living in poverty or facing economic hardship. For example, a self-help book might advise readers to "follow their passion" and turn their hobbies into careers. While this might be feasible for someone with a financial safety net, it is far less realistic for someone struggling to make ends meet who cannot afford to take risks. The advice to "just do what you love" ignores many people's harsh economic realities, including the need for stable employment, healthcare, and a living wage. It also overlooks the fact that economic inequality is not simply a matter of individual choice but is deeply entrenched in structural factors such as access to education, labour market discrimination, and monetary policy (Piketty, 2014).

The self-help industry's emphasis on personal responsibility can perpetuate the stigma associated with poverty and economic disadvantage. By framing success as a matter of individual effort, the industry reinforces the notion that those struggling are simply not trying hard enough. This narrative is particularly damaging because it shifts the focus away from the systemic causes of poverty, such as wage stagnation, lack of affordable housing, and the decline of unions, and instead places the blame on individuals. It also contributes to the myth of meritocracy, the idea that anyone can achieve success if they work hard enough, which justifies existing inequalities and limits support for policies that address economic injustice (Soss, Fording, & Schram, 2011). The self-help industry's neglect of social, cultural, and economic factors is not just an oversight – it reflects the broader ideological context in which it operates. The industry is deeply embedded in neoliberal ideology, emphasising individualism, free markets, and limited government intervention. Neoliberalism posits that individuals are rational actors who are responsible for their outcomes and that social problems can be solved through personal responsibility and market-based solutions. This ideology is evident in the self-help narrative, which promotes the idea that individuals can overcome obstacles through determination, resilience, and the right mindset. This narrative is fundamentally flawed because it ignores the structural factors constraining individual choices and limiting opportunities. It also fails to recognise that not all individuals have the same access to resources, power, and opportunities and that these inequalities are often rooted in social, cultural, and economic systems that go far beyond the control of any one person. As Harvey (2005) argues, neoliberalism has reconfigured the concept of citizenship to emphasise self-reliance and individual responsibility, effectively shifting the burden of social problems from the state to the individual. This shift has profound implications for understanding and addressing social issues, as it obscures the need for collective action and systemic change. The self-help industry's focus on individualism also has psychological consequences, particularly for those unable to achieve the promised success.

The emphasis on personal responsibility can lead to guilt, shame, and inadequacy when individuals cannot overcome the systemic barriers they face. This is particularly true for marginalised individuals who are told they can succeed if they work harder, think more positively, or adopt the right habits. When these efforts fail to produce the desired results, the blame is placed squarely on the individual, reinforcing that they are somehow deficient or lacking in willpower (Lilienfeld, 2007). The self-help industry's neglect of social, cultural, and economic factors can exacerbate the very problems it claims to address. For example, the focus on individualism can lead to social isolation, as individuals are encouraged to prioritise their own needs and goals above those of others. This can undermine the social support networks that are crucial for coping with stress, managing mental health, and achieving well-being. Similarly, the emphasis on personal responsibility can perpetuate the stigma associated with poverty, mental distress, and other social issues, making it more difficult for individuals to seek help and support.

In exploring the human condition, we encounter the uniqueness of each experience that defies simple solutions or straightforward narratives. The self-help industry, with its seductive promise of easy answers and universal formulae, often fails to capture this complexity. Instead, it offers a "one-size-fits-all" approach that oversimplifies the human experience and overlooks the profound impact of social, cultural, and economic factors on our lives. By promoting the idea that personal success and fulfilment are entirely within the individual's control, the industry ignores the systemic barriers many face and perpetuates harmful myths about personal responsibility. To suggest that a universal approach can address the diverse challenges that arise from this complexity is to ignore the very nature of what it means to be human. We are not isolated beings operating in a vacuum; we are deeply interconnected within our communities, influenced by our societies, and shaped by forces beyond our control. By ignoring the broader context in which people live, the industry offers solutions that are often inadequate and reinforces societal structures that perpetuate inequality and injustice. Personal growth and societal change require more than individual effort; they demand an understanding of the intricate interplay between personal agency and the social, cultural, and economic forces that shape our lives. As we move forward, it is essential to recognise that addressing the challenges of the human condition requires a more holistic approach – one that acknowledges the uniqueness of human existence and the need for collective action and systemic change. By doing so, we can create a more just and equitable society where the constraints of one's environment do not limit the potential for personal fulfilment but are nurtured and supported by the community. In this way, we can move beyond the oversimplifications of the self-help industry and embrace a more nuanced understanding of living in contentment.

For example, the mantra "Good Vibes Only" is as ubiquitous as Wi-Fi. Toxic positivity has become the cultural equivalent of that overly enthusiastic friend who insists everything is fine – even when it's not. No matter the circumstances, this relentless pressure to maintain an upbeat, cheery outlook might seem harmless, and even beneficial. After all, who wouldn't want to be happier, more resilient, and perpetually positive? Yet, beneath the surface of this feel-good "philosophy" lies a more insidious impact on mental health and well-being. Consider the widespread cultural phenomenon of social media influencers, often portraying a life of unending joy, success, and fulfilment. With their perfectly curated feeds, these influencers usually promote a lifestyle where negativity is absent, and every challenge is met with a smile and a motivational quote: " You got this." However, the pressure to conform to this idealised life version can lead to a dissonance between how individuals feel and how they think they should feel. Exposure to such content can lead to negative self-comparisons, where individuals believe their lives are less fulfilling or successful than those they see online, contributing to feelings of inadequacy and depression.

Toxic positivity invalidates emotions like sadness. Imagine someone going through a difficult time – perhaps dealing with the loss of a loved one, a breakup, or a significant career setback – and being told to "Think positive" or "You got this". These platitudes, though well-intentioned, can be detrimental. They suggest that the person's negative emotions are not valid or worth expressing, and they impose an unrealistic standard that one should always be happy. Suppressing negative emotions, however, doesn't make them go away. It can make them more intense. As Brene Brown (2018) puts it, "Numbing vulnerability is especially debilitating because it doesn't just deaden the pain of shame, it also deadens the pain of joy, belonging, creativity, and empathy." In other words, by pushing away negative emotions, we also dull our ability to experience positive ones, creating a paradox where the pursuit of constant happiness leads to a diminished capacity for joy.

Toxic positivity also perpetuates an unhelpful narrative around mental health: the idea that mental health challenges can be overcome simply by "thinking positively" or "choosing happiness". This narrative is too reductive, as it places the burden of recovery on the individual's mindset, ignoring the interplay of biological, psychological, and social factors that contribute to mental distress. In many corporate environments, there's an unspoken expectation that employees should maintain a positive, "can-do" attitude at all times, regardless of the stress or pressure they might be under. This can create a toxic work culture where employees cannot voice their concerns or admit to feeling overwhelmed. Moreover, toxic positivity can undermine genuine social connections. The expectation to "stay positive" can stifle meaningful conversations about difficult experiences. When one partner in a relationship, for example, is struggling with a challenging situation and is met with toxic positivity – responses like "Just think positive" or "It could be worse" – they may feel misunderstood and unsupported. This can lead to isolation, as they might conclude that their feelings are not valid or important enough to share. Over time, this can erode trust and intimacy in relationships, as individuals feel they must hide their true selves to conform to the expectation of perpetual positivity.

Popular culture often reinforces this mindset, particularly in the self-help industry, where books, seminars, and social media influencers frequently promote the idea that happiness and success are simply a matter of choosing the right attitude. While appealing, this message is overly simplistic. It ignores the reality that life is inherently filled with ups and downs and that experiencing a full range of emotions is ordinary and necessary for personal growth and well-being. As a result, toxic positivity becomes a form of emotional bypassing, where difficult emotions are ignored or swept under the rug rather than being processed and understood. The solution to toxic positivity is not embracing negativity or wallowing in despair but accepting a more balanced and authentic range of emotions and psychological states. It also means creating spaces – both in personal relationships and society – where people can be open about their feelings without fear of judgement or invalidation. Doing so can cultivate a culture that values emotional authenticity over superficial positivity.

# Chapter 3

# Tyranny of Optimism

## Toxic Positivity

In the vibrant screen scrolling of contemporary culture, where mobile phone camera filters add a rosy hue to life's most mundane moments, and motivational quotes are plastered across most social media feeds, there lies a concept that, while well-intentioned, has morphed into a psychologically insidious phenomenon: toxic positivity. This is the belief that no matter how dire or distressing a situation, one must maintain a positive mindset, as if negativity is an insult to the modern pursuit of happiness. While positivity is a valuable trait – encouraging resilience and hope – it becomes toxic when it demands unwavering cheerfulness at the expense of authentic emotional experiences. Toxic positivity is the cultural pressure to always be happy and optimistic, regardless of the reality of one's circumstances, leading to the suppression of genuine emotions and, paradoxically, to an increased burden of psychological distress.

Constant positivity seems benign, even desirable. Who wouldn't prefer to face life's challenges with a smile rather than a scowl? However, the insistence on unrelenting positivity can be profoundly damaging. It invalidates the full spectrum of human emotions, particularly those deemed negative, such as sadness, anger, or grief. These emotions, though uncomfortable, are natural responses to life's adversities and are essential for psychological processing and healing. Forcing positivity in the face of genuine emotional pain can prevent individuals from confronting and working through their feelings, leading to emotional repression and a sense of isolation. As Brown (2018) points out, "Numbing the dark doesn't stop the light – it just makes it all go numb." In other words, when we suppress our negative emotions, we do not just eliminate the bad; we dull our capacity to experience the good as well.

The roots of toxic positivity can be traced back to the broader cultural obsession with happiness and success. In a society that reveres individual achievement and views failure as a personal flaw, negativity must be avoided at all costs. This cultural narrative is reinforced by the self-help industry, which often peddles the idea that success and happiness are simply a matter of maintaining the right attitude. Popular books like Norman Vincent Peale's *The Power of Positive Thinking* (2012) have long promoted the idea that a positive mental attitude can overcome any obstacle, a notion that, while empowering in theory, fails to account for the complexities of real-life struggles. This overly simplistic view of positivity overlooks the reality that not all problems can be solved by simply thinking positive thoughts; some challenges require more than just a shift in mindset – they require systemic change, professional intervention, or simply the passage of time.

Toxic positivity can be particularly harmful when applied to mental health. The pressure to remain upbeat can lead individuals to minimise or ignore their psychological distress, preventing them from seeking the help they need. This is worth noting in the context of depression and anxiety, where the expectation to "just stay positive" can worsen feelings of guilt and inadequacy. When someone is experiencing mental health distress, telling them "To be grateful" can be not only unhelpful but also damaging. It suggests that their distress is the result of their failure to maintain a positive attitude rather than acknowledging their condition. Ehrenreich (2009) argues that the insistence on positivity can create a culture of blame, where those who cannot gather a cheerful disposition are seen as solely responsible for their experience.

The problem with toxic positivity is not just that it dismisses negative emotions but that it also imposes an unrealistic standard of happiness. This pressure to be constantly positive can lead to what some call the "tyranny of positivity", where individuals feel compelled to present an image of perpetual happiness, even when struggling. This can be particularly prevalent on social media, where the pressure to curate a perfect life can lead to a disconnect between how people present themselves online and how they feel. The result is a culture where authenticity is sacrificed for appearance, leading to increased feelings of loneliness and inadequacy. Studies have shown that the discrepancy between one's real life and one's online persona can contribute to feelings of depression and anxiety (Chou & Edge, 2012). When everyone else appears to be living their best life, the pressure to conform can be overwhelming, leaving individuals feeling isolated.

Toxic positivity also has significant implications for how we respond to others in times of distress. To comfort or support, we might resort to platitudes like "Everything happens for a reason" or "It could be worse", which, while well-meaning, can invalidate the other person's experience. These statements, often rooted in a desire to fix or solve rather than to listen and understand, can make the individual feel like their feelings are being dismissed or minimised. Offering such simplistic reassurances can undermine the process of emotional validation, which is crucial for healing (Rogers, 1961). Genuine empathy involves sitting with someone in their pain, acknowledging their feelings, and offering support without trying to change or "fix" them. Toxic positivity, on the other hand, demands that the person in pain conform to a narrative of optimism, which can leave them feeling even more alone.

In the workplace, toxic positivity can manifest as a culture where only positive feedback is welcome, and negative emotions or critiques are discouraged. This can create an environment where employees cannot express their true feelings or concerns, leading to burnout, decreased job satisfaction, and a lack of innovation. When negative emotions are suppressed in favour of a constant "can-do" attitude, problems are not addressed and underlying issues fester. This can be particularly problematic in high-stress professions, where the pressure to maintain a positive attitude can prevent individuals from seeking the support they need. As Fisher (2017) suggests, a workplace culture prioritising positivity over authenticity can harm individual well-being and organisational health.

In the high-octane world of corporate life, the relentless pursuit of success often veils the reality of failure behind a curtain of forced optimism. This is never more apparent than in the aftermath of a botched product launch, where toxic positivity – the insidious insistence on maintaining a positive outlook at all costs – can lead to disastrous consequences. Allow me to recount a tale of a company a friend used to work at, where a launch went spectacularly wrong. Yet, the atmosphere was thick and cheerful until the inevitable crash came. It all began with what was supposed to be a groundbreaking product launch. The design team had spent countless hours perfecting every detail, the marketing department had crafted the perfect narrative, and the entire company was excited. But beneath this front of excitement, there was an undercurrent of unease. Whispers circulated that the design wasn't as original as it appeared. Rumours that the design was suspiciously similar to a competitor's had been dismissed with a wave of the hand – "Let's not focus on the negatives. Everything is good. Remember, no negativity; it reflects poorly on us."

As the launch day approached, the tension grew palpable. Yet, the company culture of enforced positivity meant no one dared voice their concerns. Remember to be positive; critical thinking is not allowed. Be a team player, be like a family. Instead, every meeting was filled with hollow affirmations, misused quotes and forced smiles. "This is going to be a game-changer!" the executives declared, despite the gnawing doubts many felt. But in a workplace where toxic positivity reigned supreme, admitting to these doubts was akin to admitting failure. And then came the launch. The product was released with much fanfare, but the aftermath was a nightmare. Within hours, it became clear that the product was, in fact, a near-identical copy of a competitor's design, and it didn't work anywhere near as well. The fallout was magically brutal. Legal threats were issued, social media erupted in outrage, and the company's reputation plummeted. But even as the reality of the situation became impossible to ignore, the leadership team clung to their mantra: "Let's keep a positive mindset. Focus on the good."

At this point, one of the managers snapped, having reached his breaking point. In a moment of unfiltered honesty, he said, "This product is shit! How can we keep pretending otherwise?" His outburst was met with a telling silence, as though he had committed the ultimate sin: being critical of the situation. But the truth had been unavoidable for some time. No positivity could obscure the fact that the launch had been a catastrophic failure. And in the weeks that followed, the consequences became all too clear. Half of the department was laid off in a desperate attempt to cut costs and salvage what was left of the company. The insistence on toxic positivity had blinded the management to the warning signs, stifled critical feedback, and led to the downfall of many talented individuals who had simply been trying to do their jobs. This anecdote tells us about the dangers of toxic positivity in the workplace. When employees are discouraged from acknowledging and addressing problems head-on, a culture that prioritises positivity over critical thinking and scepticism may seem appealing. However, it can also create an environment where action, learning, and reflection are stifled, and dissenting voices are silenced and victimised.

The relentless pursuit of positivity can lead to emotional bypassing, where individuals use positivity to avoid dealing with painful emotions. This can manifest in statements like "Just focus on the good" or "Don't dwell on the negative", which, while seemingly helpful, actually encourage individuals to bypass their true feelings. Like spiritual bypassing, emotional bypassing involves using positivity as a defence mechanism to avoid confronting difficult emotions (Masters, 2010). This can prevent individuals from fully processing their feelings and can lead to unresolved grief, anger, or sadness. In the long run, this avoidance can have detrimental effects on mental health, as suppressed emotions tend to resurface in other ways, such as physical illness or increased anxiety and depression.

Toxic positivity in the workplace is particularly problematic when viewed through groupthink. Groupthink occurs when a group prioritises unanimity and cohesion over critical analysis and diverse opinions (Janis, 1972). In a groupthink scenario, members often suppress dissenting viewpoints to avoid conflict, leading to suboptimal or even disastrous decisions. Groupthink is more likely to occur in environments with a strong desire for consensus, high group cohesion, and a directive leadership style – conditions often found in workplaces where toxic positivity prevails. When a workplace culture emphasises positivity to the exclusion of others, it can discourage employees from voicing concerns or offering contrasting viewpoints. This suppression of dissent is a hallmark of groupthink, where the desire for harmony and consensus leads to a narrow view of possible solutions (Janis, 1972). For example, in a company where toxic positivity is the norm, employees might hesitate to raise concerns about a new project or initiative, fearing that they will be seen as unfavourable or not a "team player". This can lead to poor decision-making, as critical analysis is sacrificed in favour of maintaining the appearance of optimism.

The consequences of toxic positivity and groupthink are evident in several high-profile corporate failures – where a culture of excessive optimism and uncritical consensus led to the concealment of massive financial losses. Employees can be encouraged to maintain a positive outlook and avoid questioning the company's practices, leading to a corporate culture where poor practices dominate (Tourish & Vatcha, 2005). The 1986 Challenger space shuttle disaster, where groupthink influenced the decision to launch despite known technical issues. NASA engineers who raised concerns about the O-ring seals were dismissed in favour of maintaining a positive outlook and proceeding with the launch as planned. This failure to critically evaluate the risks, driven by a desire to avoid conflict and adhere to the schedule, might have resulted in the tragic loss of seven astronauts (Esser & Lindoerfer, 1989). The toxic positivity surrounding the mission's success and the pressure to conform to a group consensus contributed to a fatal decision. Several psychological mechanisms contribute to the reinforcement of toxic positivity within a groupthink context. One such mechanism is the illusion of invulnerability, where group members develop an inflated sense of confidence in the group's decisions and capabilities (Janis, 1972). This illusion can be exacerbated in a workplace culture dominated by toxic positivity, as employees are discouraged from acknowledging potential risks or failures. The result is a collective blindness to the possibility of error leading to reckless decision-making. A further mechanism is the self-censorship of dissenting opinions, where individuals withhold their concerns or criticisms to avoid disrupting the group's harmony. In a toxic positivity culture, this self-censorship is reinforced by the belief that opposing or critical viewpoints are unwelcome. Employees may fear being labelled as pessimistic, uncooperative, or not behaving as part of the family if they voice their concerns. This leads to a situation where only positive, agreeable opinions are expressed, further entrenching the groupthink dynamic (Hart, 1991). The presence of mind guards – individuals who take it upon themselves to protect the group from dissenting information – is another feature of groupthink that can be intensified by toxic positivity. These mind guards may actively discourage the expression of negative opinions or shield the group from information contradicting the prevailing optimistic narrative. In doing so, they create an echo chamber where only positive feedback is heard, and critical issues are ignored (Janis, 1972).

Toxic positivity is not just an individual issue; it is also a societal one. The cultural insistence on positivity can prevent us from acknowledging and addressing systemic problems, such as racism, inequality, and environmental degradation. When we insist on focusing only on the positive, we may overlook the real issues that must be addressed. This can create a culture of complacency, where individuals are encouraged to look on the bright side rather than advocate for change. As Hooks (2000) argues, a culture prioritising positivity over justice can complicate maintaining the status quo. We may inadvertently silence those suffering and prevent meaningful social change by insisting that individuals possess a positive attitude.

We grapple with an insidious cultural force – the Tyranny of Optimism. This phenomenon is where the pressure to maintain a ceaselessly positive outlook on life is so pervasive that it marginalises authentic emotional experiences, fosters superficiality, and ultimately breeds a culture of emotional dishonesty. While optimism can be a powerful tool for resilience and motivation, when enforced as a cultural norm, it can become tyrannical, suppressing the human experience and silencing the emotions that make us whole. The tyranny of optimism is not just a personal burden but a societal force that shapes our collective psyche, often to our detriment.

Broadly speaking, tyranny is a form of government or rule where power is held by a single person or a small group who exercises it oppressively or unjustly, often without regard for the law, justice, or the rights of individuals. In historical contexts, tyranny typically refers to a regime where the ruler, known as a tyrant, seizes power illegally or by force and governs with absolute authority, often disregarding the welfare of the populace and ruling through fear, coercion, and violence. The concept of tyranny can also be applied more broadly beyond government. It can describe any situation where power is exercised in a cruel, oppressive, or unjust way, whether in politics, organisations, or even social and cultural contexts. For example, "the tyranny of the majority" refers to a situation in a democracy where the majority enforces its will on the minority in an oppressive way or disregards minority rights. Today, tyranny often connotes a severe power imbalance, where those in control impose their will without checks and balances, leading to widespread suffering, the suppression of dissent, and the denial of fundamental freedoms.

The tyranny of optimism refers to the overwhelming and pervasive expectation that individuals must always maintain a positive outlook, regardless of their circumstances. This form of tyranny emerges when the cultural and social pressures to be optimistic become so dominant that they suppress genuine emotional expression, critical thinking, and the whole experience of the human condition. In this context, optimism is not simply encouraged as a healthy mindset but is imposed as a normative standard, leading to various negative consequences.

In many societies, particularly in the West, there is a deep-seated cultural emphasis on positivity and the belief that maintaining a positive attitude is the key to success and happiness. This is reflected in popular media, self-help literature, and social norms that glorify success stories of individuals who "overcame all odds" through sheer optimism and perseverance.

The underlying message is that positive thinking is beneficial and mandatory for a fulfilling life. The tyranny of optimism leads to the suppression of negative emotions such as sadness, anger, or fear. People are often discouraged from expressing these emotions openly, as they are seen as signs of weakness or failure. This suppression can prevent individuals from processing and addressing their true feelings, leading to emotional repression and mental health issues. Social media and popular culture perpetuate an idealised version of life where everyone is constantly happy, successful, and thriving. This creates immense pressure on individuals to conform to these unrealistic standards. The fear of being judged or ostracised for not being "positive enough" reinforces the tyranny, as people feel compelled to hide their actual experiences.

The tyranny of optimism can lead to the dismissal or trivialisation of legitimate struggles and challenges. When the prevailing narrative insists that a positive mindset can overcome any obstacle, it minimises the impact of systemic issues such as poverty, discrimination, or mental illness. Individuals who face these challenges may feel blamed for their circumstances, as the focus is on their perceived lack of optimism rather than on the structural barriers they face. In an environment dominated by the tyranny of optimism, critical thinking and constructive criticism are often discouraged. Questioning the status quo or expressing doubts can be seen as negativity or pessimism, which are unwelcome in a culture that prioritises positive vibes. This stifles meaningful dialogue and prevents the exploration of issues that require more than just a positive outlook to solve them. The tyranny of optimism can strain personal relationships and community bonds. When individuals feel they must always be positive, they may find it challenging to connect authentically with others, leading to superficial interactions and a lack of deep emotional support. Communities that enforce strict norms of optimism may also overlook the needs of their most vulnerable members, as addressing these needs might involve confronting uncomfortable truths. The tyranny of optimism perpetuates inequality by shifting the focus from systemic change to individual attitudes. It suggests that anyone can succeed if they are positive enough, ignoring the structural factors that limit opportunities for many people. This narrative upholds the status quo and diverts attention from the need for collective action to address social and economic injustices.

The relentless push towards optimism is perhaps most vividly embodied in popular culture, where positivity is often commodified and sold as a universal solution to life's challenges. Consider the ubiquitous presence of motivational speakers, whose high-energy seminars promise life-changing transformations through the power of positive thinking. Robbins's brand of optimism is seductive, offering a clear and straightforward path to success: change your mindset, and the world will change with you. However, while empowering on the surface, this narrative oversimplifies the uniqueness of human experience and places an undue burden on individuals to "fix" themselves, regardless of their circumstances. This optimism is also evident in the self-help industry, which churns out bestseller books that promise readers the keys to unlocking their full potential through the sheer force of will. These texts promote a vision of life where positivity is encouraged and demanded, suggesting that negative thoughts or emotions are barriers to success. This perspective is not only reductive but also inherently dismissive of the real struggles that people face, whether financial hardships, health crises, or systemic injustices. By framing optimism as the ultimate virtue, these cultural products imply that failure to thrive results from a lack of positivity.

The tyranny of optimism is further reinforced by social media platforms like Instagram, where the curated perfection of influencers' lives creates an illusion of constant happiness and success. The #GoodVibesOnly movement, for example, has become a rallying cry for those who seek to banish negativity from their lives, often at the cost of authenticity. In this digital landscape, there is little room for vulnerability or struggle; instead, users are encouraged to present an airbrushed version of reality where every setback is a setup for a comeback, and every challenge is an opportunity for growth. This relentless positivity, however, can lead to a profound sense of inadequacy and alienation as individuals compare their messy, imperfect lives to the unattainable ideals they see online (Chou & Edge, 2012). The tyranny of optimism is not just a cultural phenomenon; it has significant psychological consequences. This can result in increased stress, and even depression, as people feel isolated in their inability to live up to the unrealistic standards set by society (Fisher, 2017). In a culture that reveres positivity, there is little space for authentic expression of pain, anger, or sadness, leading to a disconnect between inner and outer experiences.

The tyranny of optimism also manifests in the workplace, where the expectation to maintain a positive attitude can create a toxic environment. The corporate world often promotes the idea that success results directly from a positive mindset, leading to a culture where employees feel pressured to hide their true feelings and concerns. This can lead to burnout, as individuals push themselves to maintain a vibe of positivity even when overwhelmed or dissatisfied. The emphasis on positivity can also stifle creativity and innovation, as employees may be reluctant to voice dissenting opinions or express doubts for fear of being labelled as "negative" or "not a team player" (Fisher, 2017). Popular culture often exacerbates the tyranny of optimism by promoting a narrative of individual responsibility that ignores the broader social and economic forces. This is most evident in the portrayal of success in films and television shows, where characters who achieve their dreams are often depicted as having done so through sheer determination and a positive attitude. The underlying message is clear: if you are unsuccessful, it is because you did not try hard enough or did not think positively enough. This narrative, while inspirational to some, can be profoundly alienating to those who face structural barriers to success, such as poverty, discrimination, or lack of access to education and resources (Giroux, 2008). The tyranny of optimism also has political implications, as it can be used to justify the status quo and discourage collective action. By promoting the idea that an individual mindset is the key to success, this cultural force shifts the focus away from systemic issues. It places the burden of change on the individual. This is evident in the "bootstrap" ideology rhetoric, which suggests that anyone can succeed if they work hard enough and maintain a positive attitude, regardless of obstacles. This narrative conveniently ignores the role of structural inequality and the need for social and political change, instead placing the blame for failure squarely on the shoulders of the individual (Harvey, 2005). In mental health, the tyranny of optimism can be particularly concerning. The pressure to remain positive can prevent individuals from seeking help or acknowledging their struggles, leading to a culture of silence around mental distress. The stigma surrounding mental health issues is often exacerbated by the expectation to "stay strong" and "keep a positive attitude", which can discourage individuals from expressing their true feelings or seeking the support they need (Ehrenreich, 2009).

The relentless push towards optimism also raises important ethical questions about the role of media and influencers in shaping public perceptions of happiness and success. The commodification of positivity has created a lucrative market for self-help books, motivational seminars, and wellness products, all of which promise to help individuals achieve a "good life" through positive thinking. However, this emphasis on positivity often overlooks the complexity of human experience and the reality that not all problems can be solved by simply changing one's mindset. Focusing on individual responsibility can also divert attention away from the need for collective action and systemic change, reinforcing existing power structures and perpetuating inequality (Illouz, 2008). The tyranny of optimism, with its insistence on perpetual positivity, undermines the richness of the human experience. Life is not always sunshine and rainbows; it is also filled with challenges, disappointments, and losses that require more than just a positive attitude to navigate. By enforcing a narrow definition of happiness and success, this cultural force denies individuals the opportunity to fully engage with their emotions and experiences, both positive and negative. It also perpetuates a culture of superficiality, where the appearance of happiness is valued more than genuine well-being.

## Good Vibes Only

In an era where social media captions preach resilience and viral dances are set to "Don't Worry, Be Happy", our culture has developed an unhealthy obsession with positivity. Like a trendy filter applied to human emotions, toxic positivity has become the social mandate of the twenty-first century. But this relentless push to "stay positive" at all costs does more than annoy those having a bad day – it actively invalidates their emotions, turning human experience into a stifling monoculture of enforced cheerfulness. Overgeneralising a happy, optimistic state results in the denial, minimisation, and invalidation of the authentic human emotional experience. The mindset encourages people to dismiss their feelings and those of others in favour of an imaginary, often unattainable, constant state of happiness.

Consider the ubiquitous phrase, "Good vibes only", a mantra adopted by everyone from fitness influencers to corporate wellness programmes. While it seems harmless – who would not prefer good vibes over bad ones? – this phrase is emblematic of a broader societal trend that discourages the expression of anything other than happiness or positivity. It sends the message that there is no room for negativity, discomfort, criticality or struggle and, by extension, no room for the people experiencing those genuine emotions. One of the most glaring examples of toxic positivity in popular culture is the proliferation of social media influencers who curate their lives to present an image of flawless happiness and perpetual success. These platforms have become breeding grounds for this type of content, where the pressure to present an idealised version of oneself can suppress any emotion that does not fit into the perfectly filtered frame. This relentless positivity is not only unrealistic but also harmful, as it engineers a culture where individuals feel compelled to hide their struggles and put on a happy face, even when they're not happy. Research by Chou and Edge (2012) suggests that social media use can lead to negative self-comparisons and feelings of inadequacy, particularly when users are constantly bombarded with images of others' seemingly perfect lives.

The detrimental nature of toxic positivity lies in its ability to make people feel guilty or ashamed for having perfectly normal human reactions to life's challenges. Imagine, for example, someone who has just lost a loved one. The natural and healthy response to such a loss is grief and painful emotion that needs to be processed over time. However, in a culture dominated by toxic positivity, this person might be told to "focus on the good times" or to "be strong", effectively minimising their grief and pressuring them to bypass their real emotions. This not only invalidates their experience but can also lead to unresolved grief, as the person is denied the space and support to process their loss fully. The expectation to remain positive in the face of adversity can lead to what psychologists' term "emotional bypassing", where individuals use positivity to avoid uncomfortable or painful emotions. This can be seen in popular self-help mantras that encourage people to "choose happiness" or "let it go" without addressing the underlying issues that may be causing the distress. While these sayings may be intended to uplift, they can instead serve as a form of emotional gaslighting, making individuals question the validity of their feelings and pushing them to suppress emotions that are crucial for their well-being. As Brown (2018) notes, the numbing of emotions does not discriminate – it numbs both the negative and positive, leading to a diminished capacity to experience joy and connection.

Toxic positivity is also prevalent in the workplace, where the expectation to maintain a positive attitude can be particularly damaging. In many corporate environments, employees are encouraged – or even required – to adopt a "can-do" attitude, regardless of their challenges. This can create a culture where legitimate concerns are dismissed, and employees feel pressured to suppress their true feelings. This is especially problematic in high-stress environments, where the pressure to remain upbeat can prevent individuals from seeking help or addressing the root causes of their stress. Fisher (2017) argues that toxic positivity can lead to burnout and decreased job satisfaction, as employees are forced to conform to an unrealistic standard of constant positivity. Toxic positivity can have significant implications for well-being, particularly for those experiencing conditions like depression or anxiety. When individuals are told to "just think positive" or "look on the bright side", it minimises their lived experiences. It places the burden of recovery solely on their ability to adopt a positive mindset. This can discourage them from seeking professional support. Depression and anxiety are mental distress experiences that, at times, require comprehensive formulations and social support – not just a shift in attitude. Ehrenreich (2009) criticises the cultural obsession with positivity for creating a climate where individuals feel pressured to mask their struggles and conform to a narrow definition of mental health and well-being, one that prioritises cheerfulness over authenticity.

In popular culture, the representation of mental health often reflects this bias towards positivity. Films and television shows frequently depict characters who overcome their mental distress through sheer willpower or a sudden change in perspective, reinforcing the idea that positivity is the key to overcoming adversity. While these narratives can be inspiring, they also risk oversimplifying mental health and promoting the harmful belief that recovery is solely a matter of mindset. This can lead to a lack of understanding and empathy for those struggling, as their experiences are dismissed as simply a failure to "stay positive", Toxic positivity also has broader societal implications, particularly in shaping our collective response to social and political issues. In the face of systemic injustices like racism, poverty, or climate change, the insistence on positivity can serve as a form of denial, preventing individuals and communities from fully grappling with the socio-political realities of these issues. The phrase "stay positive" becomes a tool of complacency, encouraging people to focus on personal development while ignoring the more significant structural problems that contribute to social inequity. Hooks (2000) argues that a culture that prioritises positivity over justice can become complicit in maintaining the status quo, as it shifts the focus away from collective action and towards individual resilience.

This phenomenon is evident in the rise of wellness culture, where pursuing personal happiness and health is often framed as the goal, excluding broader social issues. The wellness industry, which includes everything from yoga classes to dietary supplements, has commodified well-being, promoting a health vision rooted in individualism and consumerism. For example, the emphasis on mindfulness and self-care as solutions to stress can distract from the structural factors that contribute to stress, such as economic inequality, job insecurity, and social isolation

(Illouz, 2008). The commodification of positivity in the wellness industry also reinforces the idea that happiness and well-being are products to be bought and sold rather than experiences to be cultivated through meaningful relationships and community engagement. This can lead to a superficial approach to mental health, where the focus is on achieving a particular image of wellness – often depicted in the form of a serene, smiling individual – rather than on addressing the underlying causes of distress. This superficiality is evident in the rise of "positivity influencers" on social media, who promote a highly curated and brand-sponsored version of their lives that emphasises happiness and success, often at the expense of authenticity. The pressure to conform to this ideal can lead to feelings of inadequacy and disconnection as individuals struggle to live up to an unattainable standard (Chou & Edge, 2012).

Toxic positivity can also dominate relationships, where the expectation to "be positive" can hinder authentic communication and emotional connection. When individuals feel pressured to maintain a positive outlook, they may be reluctant to share their feelings with others, leading to a lack of emotional intimacy. As a result, relationships can become strained, as individuals cannot fully express themselves or receive the support they need. Furthermore, toxic positivity can perpetuate a cycle of emotional invalidation, where individuals feel pressured to suppress their negative emotions and present a positive front, even when they are in pain. This can lead to isolation, as individuals think their feelings are invalid or worthy of attention. Over time, this can contribute to loneliness and despair as individuals become disconnected from their feelings and community. Brown (2018) argues that vulnerability is essential for authentic connection, as it allows individuals to express their true selves and build meaningful relationships. However, toxic positivity discourages vulnerability, creating a culture where emotional honesty is devalued.

Bright-siding or focusing exclusively on the positive aspects of a situation while disregarding or minimising the negative is rooted in the broader cultural belief that positivity equates to personal success and well-being. This belief is pervasive in self-help literature, corporate wellness programmes, and everyday interactions. One of the most significant drawbacks of toxic positivity is its propensity to invalidate legitimate emotions. When individuals are consistently encouraged to "look on the bright side" or "stay positive", their genuine feelings of distress, sadness, or frustration are often dismissed or deemed inappropriate, due to the failure to recognise that negative emotions are part of life. According to Linehan (1993), validation involves acknowledging and accepting one's emotional experiences as legitimate. When people are told to ignore their negative feelings or that "things could be worse", they may have to suppress their emotions rather than process and address them (Cohen, 2004). The prevalence of bright-siding in corporate environments and social media further highlights its problematic nature. In corporate culture, a relentless focus on positivity can create a superficial work environment where employees are discouraged from expressing concerns and may feel compelled to mask their true feelings, leading to burnout and diminished morale.

In the long term, the impact of toxic positivity on mental health can be profound. When individuals are unable to express their negative emotions, they may turn to unhealthy coping mechanisms to manage their distress. In contrast, a culture that values emotional authenticity and encourages individuals to express their full range of emotions can support an increased sense of well-being, as individuals can process their feelings healthily and receive the support they need. I am not arguing for embracing negativity but cultivating a more balanced and authentic emotional approach that allows for a broader range of human experiences. This means recognising that all positive and negative emotions are valuable and essential to our knowledge. It means creating spaces where individuals can express their feelings without fear of judgement or invalidation and where vulnerability is seen as a strength rather than a weakness. It also means challenging cultural narratives that prioritise positivity at the expense of authenticity and advocating for a more nuanced understanding of mental health and well-being.

## Lack of Evidence

Self-help books line bookstore shelves and feature prominently on bestseller lists, with titles often suggesting that they hold the key to unlocking one's true potential. However, despite their widespread popularity, most self-help books lack robust scientific evidence to support their claims. This disconnect between popularity and empirical validity raises concerns about the efficacy of self-help literature and its potential impact on readers. The appeal of self-help books lies in their promise of quick fixes and easy solutions to life's problems. They often employ a tone of authority, with authors presenting themselves as experts who have discovered a unique formula for success. Yet, when we examine these claims through the lens of scientific inquiry, a different picture emerges – one of generalisations, anecdotal evidence, and, in many cases, pseudoscience. Many self-help books rely on the author's experiences, which, while compelling, do not constitute scientific evidence (Lilienfeld, 2007). The absence of rigorous peer-reviewed research to substantiate the advice given in these books is a glaring issue that cannot be overlooked.

One of the most significant criticisms of self-help books is their tendency to oversimplify psychological concepts. Take, for example, the idea of positive thinking. Books such as *The Power of Positive Thinking* (1952) have been a staple of the self-help genre for decades, preaching that optimism can overcome any obstacle. While positive thinking might improve one's outlook, scientific evidence does not support the idea that it alone can transform lives. Research in psychology suggests that while a positive mindset can be beneficial, it is not a panacea. For instance, a meta-analysis by Coyne and Tennen (2010) found that the benefits of positive thinking are often overstated and may even be detrimental in specific contexts, such as when it leads individuals to ignore real problems or fail to seek necessary medical treatment. Another pervasive issue in self-help literature is the promotion of methods that have not been scientifically validated. Many self-help books advocate for techniques such as visualisation, affirmations, or the law of attraction, which posit that thinking positively will bring about positive outcomes in life. These ideas, though popular, are not grounded in scientific evidence. The law of attraction, in particular, has been widely criticised by psychologists for lacking empirical support. A study by Shafran and Rachman (2004) on thought-action fusion – a concept related to the law of attraction – found that merely thinking about something does not make it more likely to occur. Despite this, some books continue to propagate the idea that the universe will conspire to deliver one's desires simply through the power of thought. This notion is more magical thinking than psychology.

Psychological research has consistently shown that interventions must be tailored to the individual to be effective (Norcross and Hill, 2002). What works for one person may not work for another due to differences in personality, cultural background, and life experiences. For example, cognitive-behavioural therapy (CBT) has been seen as effective for treating depression and anxiety, but it is not a universal remedy; some individuals respond better to other therapeutic approaches, such as psychodynamic therapy or interpersonal therapy (Cuijpers et al., 2016). Self-help books that offer generic advice without acknowledging these nuances risk being ineffective or harmful to certain readers.

The lack of scientific evidence in self-help literature can lead to the dissemination of harmful myths and misconceptions. One such myth is the idea that everyone has the power to completely control their destiny, a concept that is central to many self-help books. While personal agency is undoubtedly essential. Social psychology and sociology research have shown that socioeconomic status, education, and resource access significantly determine life outcomes. By focusing exclusively on individual responsibility, self-help books can perpetuate a blame-the-victim mentality, where those who fail to achieve success are seen as lacking willpower or determination rather than being hindered by structural inequalities.

Unlike medical treatments, which must undergo rigorous testing and approval processes before being made available to the public, self-help books face no such scrutiny. Authors can make bold claims without needing evidence, and there is no mechanism to ensure that the advice they dispense is safe or effective. This lack of regulation means that consumers (who are, at times, vulnerable people) are left to navigate a minefield of potentially misleading or harmful information. In contrast, evidence-based psychological treatments, such as those provided by licensed therapists, are subject to strict ethical guidelines and are grounded in scientific research.

The impact of self-help books on mental health is a particularly concerning issue. While some readers may find comfort or motivation in these books, others may feel inadequate or disillusioned when the promised results fail to materialise. A study by Cuijpers and Schuurmans (2007) found that self-help interventions often do not produce the same benefit as professional therapy. The gap between expectation and reality can lead to increased distress. Furthermore, the emphasis on quick fixes in many self-help books can discourage individuals from seeking professional help, as they may feel they should be able to solve their problems independently. This is particularly dangerous for individuals struggling with serious mental health distress, such as depression or anxiety, where timely and evidence-based interventions are crucial.

In addition to their lack of scientific validity, self-help books often promote a culture of relentless self-optimisation that can be psychologically exhausting. The idea that one must always be striving to improve, to be more productive, positive, and successful, can lead to exhaustion and inadequacy. This phenomenon is closely related to what psychologist Barry Schwartz (2004) refers to as the "paradox of choice", where the abundance of options and the pressure to make the "right" choice can lead to decision paralysis and dissatisfaction. In the context of self-help, the constant pursuit of self-improvement can create a never-ending cycle of striving and failing, where the reader feels that they are never good enough. It is also important to consider the ethical implications of the self-help industry's focus on monetising personal development. The commodification of self-help has led to the proliferation of products and services that promise life-changing results, often at a significant cost. Motivational seminars, online courses, and personal coaching sessions can cost thousands of pounds. Yet, there is little evidence to suggest that they are more effective than more affordable, evidence-based treatments. The high price tag associated with these products raises questions about accessibility and the exploitation of vulnerable individuals who are seeking help. Moreover, the emphasis on consumerism within the self-help industry – where the solution to one's problems is often framed as purchasing the next book, course, or product – reinforces the notion that self-worth is tied to material success.

The lack of scientific evidence in self-help books is a concern for individual readers and the broader field of psychology. The popularity of these books can perpetuate misconceptions about what psychology is and what it can offer. While psychology is grounded in rigorous scientific research, the self-help genre often presents a watered-down version of psychological principles. This can lead to a public misunderstanding of psychology. As a result, the field of psychology may struggle to gain the public's trust and differentiate itself from the pseudoscience often peddled in the self-help industry. Despite these criticisms, it is essential to acknowledge that not all self-help books are devoid of value. Some authors, such as Martin Seligman and his work on positive psychology, have made significant contributions to the field and have written popular and evidence-based books (Seligman, 2011). However, these are the exception rather than the rule. The challenge for consumers is to distinguish between self-help books that are grounded in scientific evidence and those that are not. This requires a critical eye and a willingness to question the claims made by authors rather than accepting them at face value.

# Chapter 4

# The Cult of Productivity

In today's hyper-connected, always-on world, the "more, faster, better" mantra has become a professional standard and a personal creed. This relentless pursuit of efficiency and output has given rise to what can be termed the Cult of Productivity. This phenomenon, deeply ingrained in our cultural psyche, exalts productivity as the ultimate measure of success, worth, and morality. However, beneath its surface lies a more troubling reality: the cult of productivity is unsustainable and deeply dehumanising, reducing the rich diversity of human existence to mere metrics and output. In this discussion, we will unpack this pervasive cult's origins, consequences, and ironies, drawing on psychological, sociological, and cultural critiques to explore its impact on modern life.

The origins of the cult of productivity can be traced back to the Industrial Revolution, a period that fundamentally reshaped the relationship between time, labour, and value. The shift from rural economies, where time was dictated by natural rhythms, to industrial economies, where time became a commodity, marked a profound transformation in how work was organised and valued. Max Weber's work, *The Protestant Ethic and the Spirit of Capitalism* (Weber and Kalberg, 2013), offers a critical lens through which to view this shift. Weber argues that the Protestant work ethic, with its emphasis on hard work, discipline, and frugality, laid the cultural groundwork for the rise of capitalism. In this context, productivity became not just a means to an end but a moral imperative, a sign of one's divine selection. While the religious connotations may have faded, the moralisation of productivity persists, deeply embedded in the fabric of modern capitalism. Fast forward to the twenty-

71

first century, and the cult of productivity has only intensified. The advent of digital technology, coupled with the rise of neoliberalism, has created an environment where productivity is not just encouraged but demanded. Smartphones, email, and project management tools have blurred the boundaries between work and life, leading to individuals being expected to always be productive, regardless of context. This expectation is reinforced by the gig economy, where workers are often paid by the task rather than the hour, further commodifying time and pushing the notion that every moment must be optimised for productivity.

The psychological impact of this relentless focus on productivity is profound. The constant pressure to do more and achieve more can lead to stress, burnout, and inadequacy. Research has shown that while moderate stress can enhance performance, chronic stress harms mental and physical health (APA, 2018). The rise of burnout, now recognised by the World Health Organisation as an occupational phenomenon (WHO, 2019), is a direct consequence of the cult of productivity. Burnout is characterised by emotional exhaustion, depersonalisation, and a diminished sense of personal accomplishment – all exacerbated by the unrelenting demand to be productive. In this sense, pursuing productivity can become counterproductive, leading to diminished well-being and, ironically, reduced productivity. The cult of productivity profoundly impacts how individuals perceive themselves and their worth. In a culture that prioritises output above all else, there is a tendency to equate self-worth with productivity. This is particularly evident in the rise of "hustle culture", where individuals are celebrated for their ability to juggle multiple jobs, side projects, and personal responsibilities with little regard for the toll it takes on their well-being. Social media platforms exacerbate this by creating a constant comparison loop, where individuals are bombarded with images of others' success and productivity. The result is a pervasive sense of inadequacy, as people must constantly do more to measure up.

The glorification of productivity also has significant social and cultural implications. It perpetuates a neoliberal narrative that success is solely the result of individual effort, thereby obscuring the structural factors that contribute to inequality. In this context, those who are unable to maintain high levels of productivity, whether due to illness, disability, or caregiving responsibilities, are often marginalised and stigmatised. This is particularly evident in the treatment of workers in low-wage jobs, who are usually subject to unrealistic productivity targets and harsh penalties for failing to meet them. The gig economy, where workers are often pitted against each other to complete tasks as quickly as possible, with little regard for quality or well-being, exemplifies this dynamic. The cult of productivity has infiltrated the realm of leisure, turning what should be vital activities into yet another arena for optimisation. The rise of the "productivity hack" industry, with its plethora of apps, books, and seminars promising to help individuals squeeze more value out of every moment, is a testament to this. Even activities traditionally associated with relaxation, such as yoga or meditation, are increasingly framed as tools for enhancing productivity rather than ends in themselves. This commodification of leisure reflects a broader trend towards instrumentalising all aspects of life, where every activity is judged by its potential to enhance productivity.

One of the most insidious aspects of the cult of productivity is its ability to co-opt and distort the concept of self-improvement. On the surface, the drive to be more productive appears to align with the goal of personal growth. However, the version of self-improvement promoted by the cult of productivity is often shallow and transactional, reducing personal development to a series of checkboxes to be ticked off in the quest for efficiency. This is evident in the proliferation of self-help books and courses that promise to help individuals become more productive by adopting certain habits or routines. While there is nothing inherently wrong with seeking to improve oneself, the emphasis on productivity often leads to a narrow focus on external achievements at the expense of more profound, meaningful forms of growth.

The cult of productivity also reinforces a binary view of time, where moments are either productive or wasted. This dichotomy is not only reductive but also deeply alienating, as it denies the value of activities that do not have an immediate, measurable output. For example, daydreaming, contemplation, and even boredom are essential for creativity and problem-solving, yet they are often devalued in a culture that prioritises constant activity. This is supported by research in cognitive psychology, which suggests that "mind-wandering" can enhance creativity and lead to innovative solutions (Smallwood & Schooler, 2015). By dismissing these activities as unproductive, the cult of productivity stifles creativity and narrows the range of acceptable behaviours. The focus on individual productivity often comes at the expense of collective well-being. In a culture prioritising output, there is little room for collaboration, empathy, or community. This is particularly evident in the workplace, where the pressure to be productive can lead to a competitive, cutthroat environment where individuals are pitted against each other. This not only undermines trust and cooperation but also erodes the social fabric of the workplace. In contrast, research has shown that collaborative, supportive work environments improve individual and organisational outcomes (Dutton and Ragins, 2007). By prioritising productivity over relationships, the cult of productivity undermines the very goals it seeks to achieve.

The cultural glorification of productivity also has ecological implications. The relentless pursuit of growth and efficiency often comes at the expense of the environment, as natural resources are exploited to fuel economic expansion. The logic of productivity, which emphasises maximising output, is fundamentally at odds with the need for sustainability, which requires a more measured and thoughtful approach to resource use. The environmental crisis we face today is partly a consequence of the cult of productivity, which prioritises short-term gains over long-term sustainability. Addressing this crisis requires a fundamental shift in how we think about productivity and success, moving away from a model based on endless growth towards one that values balance and sustainability. Considering these critiques, it is worth asking why the cult of productivity has such a powerful hold on our culture. One reason is that productivity is often conflated with progress at the individual and societal levels. In a capitalist economy, productivity is seen as the engine of growth and prosperity, and individuals are expected to contribute to this engine through their labour. The logic of productivity is so deeply ingrained in our cultural and economic systems that it can be difficult to imagine alternatives. However, as we have seen, this logic is not without its costs, and there is growing recognition of the need to rethink our relationship with productivity.

One antidote to the cult of productivity is the concept of "good enough", which challenges the idea that we must always strive for more. The notion of "good enough" does not mean settling for mediocrity but recognising that perfection is neither achievable nor desirable. By embracing "good enough", we can free ourselves from constant optimisation and make room for activities that may not be productive in the traditional sense but are nonetheless valuable. This might include spending time with loved ones, engaging in creative pursuits, or simply allowing ourselves to rest. Another approach is to redefine what we mean by productivity. Rather than measuring productivity solely in terms of output, we could adopt a more holistic view that considers well-being, sustainability, and social impact. This would require a fundamental shift in how we structure work and leisure, moving away from a model that prioritises efficiency at all costs towards one that values balance, creativity, and community. Such a shift would improve individual well-being and contribute to a more just and sustainable society.

## Superstitious Learning

There exists a curious parallel to one of psychology's classic experiments – the phenomenon of superstitious learning by Skinner. In the 1940s, superstitious learning was used to describe a scenario where individuals, like Skinner's famous pigeons, mistakenly link an action with an unrelated outcome due to coincidental timing (Skinner, 1948). Skinner's pigeon experiment is a foundational study in behaviourism, particularly in understanding operant conditioning. In this experiment, Skinner placed pigeons in a "Skinner box", which contained a lever or button that the pigeons could peck. When the pigeons pecked the lever, a food pellet would be delivered as a reward, reinforcing the behaviour. Through this setup, Skinner explored how different schedules of reinforcement affected the pigeons' behaviour. For example, under a continuous reinforcement schedule, the pigeons received food every time they pecked the lever, thereby quickly learning the association and stopping when the reinforcement ceased (extinction). Skinner further experimented with fixed-ratio, variable-ratio, fixed-interval, and variable-interval schedules, producing distinct behaviour patterns. A particularly intriguing aspect of the study involved "superstition" in pigeons: when food was delivered at regular intervals, regardless of the pigeons' actions, they developed repetitive behaviours, mistakenly believing that these actions influenced the arrival of food. This phenomenon highlighted how random reinforcement can lead to superstitious behaviours, offering insights into human actions in contexts like gambling or rituals. Skinner's experiment thus demonstrated how environmental factors, through reinforcement, can shape and control behaviour, underscoring the principles of operant conditioning in behaviourism. Just as a pigeon might believe that turning in circles causes food to appear, people, under the influence of self-help rituals, might believe that affirmations or routines can magically transform their lives. This phenomenon raises questions about the efficacy of the self-help industry and highlights its potential to mislead individuals into a cycle of false beliefs and unwarranted behaviours.

Superstitious learning is fundamentally about the human tendency to seek control in uncertain situations by creating connections between actions and outcomes where none exist. The self-help industry taps into this deep-seated need for control by offering seemingly foolproof methods for achieving success, happiness, and personal fulfilment. These methods often involve specific, repetitive actions – daily affirmations, visualisation exercises, or adherence to a strict regimen – purported to lead directly to the desired outcome. The problem, however, is that these methods are frequently devoid of empirical support. Instead, they rely on anecdotal success stories and the psychological comfort of routine. This can lead individuals to attribute their successes to these practices even when the connection is coincidental.

For example, consider the widespread popularity of the "law of attraction". The basic premise is that by thinking positively and focusing on one's desires, the universe will somehow conspire to bring these desires to fruition. This concept aligns closely with superstitious learning because it encourages the belief that specific thoughts or feelings can directly influence external events, much like Skinner's pigeons believed their behaviour controlled the appearance of food. The danger lies in the false sense of agency this creates. People might spend significant time and energy on these rituals, believing that they are directly influencing their fate, when their successes and failures are likely determined by an interplay of factors beyond their control.

The reliance on superstitious learning in self-help fosters a culture of magical thinking and perpetuates a significant ethical concern: the misattribution of success and failure. When individuals achieve their goals, they might credit their success to the self-help techniques they have been practising, reinforcing their belief in these methods. However, when they fail, they may be led to believe that they did not perform the rituals correctly or with enough conviction. This can create a toxic cycle of blame and self-doubt as individuals continually invest more into the self-help industry, hoping to finally "get it right", This cycle is not only emotionally draining but can also be financially exploitative, as the self-help industry profits from the endless pursuit of personal transformation (McGee, 2005).

The emphasis on superstitious learning within self-help culture can have broader social implications, particularly in regard to how it frames the narrative of personal responsibility. The core message of many self-help materials is that individuals are entirely in control of their destinies. If they are failing, they are not following the prescribed steps diligently enough. This perspective is both reductive and dangerously misleading, as it ignores the structural and systemic factors that play a significant role in determining life outcomes (Ehrenreich, 2009). By focusing solely on individual behaviour, the self-help industry perpetuates the myth that success is a matter of personal effort alone, thereby obscuring the realities of social inequality, economic barriers, and other external constraints.

The social and psychological consequences of this narrative are profound. Individuals who subscribe to these superstitious beliefs may become increasingly isolated, believing their struggles result from personal failings rather than recognising the external factors at play. This can lead to alienation and disempowerment, as the individual internalises the belief that they are solely to blame for their circumstances. Moreover, this individualistic approach undermines the importance of community and collective action in addressing societal issues. In a world where many challenges – such as economic inequality, mental health crises, and environmental degradation – require systemic solutions, the self-help industry's focus on personal empowerment can be seen as a distraction from the need for broader social change (McGee, 2005).

In addition to the psychological and social ramifications, the reliance on superstitious learning within self-help culture also raises questions about the scientific validity of these practices. Many self-help techniques are presented with the veneer of scientific legitimacy, often citing studies or using psychological jargon to bolster their claims. However, these references are frequently taken out of context, misinterpreted, or based on anecdotal evidence rather than rigorous scientific research. This pseudo-scientific approach not only misleads consumers but also undermines the credibility of the psychological profession. As Tavris (2014) argues, the proliferation of pseudoscience in self-help can contribute to a general mistrust of legitimate psychological interventions, making it more difficult for individuals to access evidence-based treatments when needed.

The emphasis on ritualistic behaviour within a self-help culture can have unintended consequences, particularly when it comes to mental health. For individuals experiencing anxiety, depression, or other mental health issues, the pressure to follow specific routines or rituals can magnify their symptoms. The belief that they must adhere to these practices to achieve success can create additional stress and anxiety, particularly if they feel they are not performing the rituals correctly. This can lead to a worsening of their mental health as they become trapped in a cycle of obsessive behaviour and self-blame. The promotion of these practices as a substitute for professional mental health care can discourage individuals from seeking the help they need, potentially delaying or preventing their recovery (Rosen, 1993).

## Everyday I'm Hustling

The hustle mentality, a way of thinking that glorifies relentless work, non-stop ambition, and the continuous pursuit of success, has permeated modern culture absurdly. It is a mindset that tells us that the key to happiness and fulfilment lies in our ability to grind harder, sleep less, and sacrifice more – all to achieve our goals. From social media influencers preaching the gospel of the 5 AM club to business moguls extolling the virtues of 100-hour workweeks, the hustle mentality has become a dominant narrative in the twenty-first century. However, as a critical observer – and a voice of reason – it is essential to question whether this mentality is a path to success or a recipe for disillusionment. The hustle mentality has been further fuelled by neoliberalism – a political and economic ideology emphasising free markets, individualism, and minimal government intervention. Under neoliberalism, the individual is seen as the architect of their destiny, responsible for their success or failure based on their work ethic and personal choices (Harvey, 2005). This ideology dovetails perfectly with the hustle mentality, which promotes the idea that success is entirely within one's control and that the key to achieving it is to work harder and longer than everyone else. The implication is clear: if you are failing, you are not hustling hard enough.

Social media has played a significant role in amplifying the hustle mentality. Social media platforms are rife with influencers and entrepreneurs showcasing their relentless grind, often accompanied by motivational quotes about the virtues of hard work. These posts create a curated image of success that is both aspirational and, at times, unattainable. The hustle mentality thrives in this environment, where the constant comparison to others exacerbates the pressure to achieve and outdo oneself constantly. It is not enough to work hard in silence; one must also broadcast their efforts to the world, further entrenching the belief that relentless work is the ultimate measure of success. However, one of the most significant dangers of the hustle mentality is its contribution to burnout. Burnout, as defined by the World Health Organisation (2019), is a syndrome resulting from chronic workplace stress that has not been successfully managed. It is characterised by feelings of energy depletion, increased mental distance from one's job, and reduced professional efficacy. With its glorification of overwork and its disdain for rest, the hustle mentality creates the perfect conditions for burnout to thrive.

Burnout can be defined as a psychological condition characterised by chronic workplace stress that has not been successfully managed. It is marked by three key dimensions: emotional exhaustion, depersonalisation, and a reduced sense of personal accomplishment (Maslach & Leiter, 2016). Emotional exhaustion refers to feeling emotionally drained and overwhelmed by one's work, leading to depleting emotional and physical resources. Depersonalisation, or cynicism, involves a detached and impersonal response towards one's job and colleagues, often manifesting as a negative or callous attitude. The reduced sense of personal accomplishment is the feeling of ineffectiveness and a lack of achievement in one's work. Burnout is not merely a temporary state of stress but a severe condition that can lead to significant mental and physical health issues, including depression, anxiety, and cardiovascular diseases (Maslach & Leiter, 2016; WHO, 2019). The World Health Organisation (WHO) recognises burnout as an "occupational phenomenon" in its International Classification of Diseases, underscoring its impact on workers' health and well-being (WHO, 2019). Addressing burnout requires organisational changes, such as reducing workload, increasing job autonomy, and providing support systems alongside individual strategies for stress management. Research in psychology supports this connection between the hustle mentality and burnout. A study by Maslach and Leiter (2016) found that excessive work demands, lack of recovery time, and the blurring of work-life boundaries – hallmarks of the hustle mentality – are significant predictors of burnout. Furthermore, the pressure to constantly hustle can lead to a lack of sleep, poor physical health, and mental exhaustion, all contributing to burnout. Moreover, burnout is not just an individual problem; it has broader implications for organisations, including decreased productivity, higher turnover rates, and increased healthcare costs.

The hustle mentality can be counterproductive despite its emphasis on productivity. The relentless focus on work can diminish returns, as individuals become less effective when tired, stressed, and burned out. Research by Amabile and Kramer (2011) on the progress principle suggests that small wins and a sense of meaningful progress are critical drivers of motivation and productivity. However, mentally emphasising constant grinding, the hustle can obscure these small wins, creating a sense of futility and frustration. Instead of fostering sustained productivity, the hustle mentality can lead to a cycle of overwork, burnout, and decreased performance.

The hustle mentality glorifies work for work's sake and ignores the importance of purpose and meaning in one's work. While hard work is undoubtedly important, it is not enough to create a fulfilling and meaningful life. The philosopher Bertrand Russell (1972) argued that the value of work lies not in the amount of effort expended, but in the quality and purpose of that work. Similarly, contemporary research on meaningful work suggests that individuals who find purpose in their work are more engaged, satisfied, and resilient (Steger et al., 2012). However, the hustle mentality's emphasis on output rather than meaning can lead to a sense of emptiness and disillusionment, as individuals work harder but do not feel more fulfilled. Given these critiques, it is worth asking whether the hustle mentality is sustainable or desirable. While the ethos of hard work and ambition is not inherently harmful, the extreme version of these values promoted by the hustle mentality is both unrealistic and unhealthy. Instead of glorifying relentless work, we should advocate for a more balanced and holistic approach to success, recognising the importance of rest, relationships, and meaning in life. One possible alternative to the hustle mentality is the "work-life integration" concept, which emphasises the importance of balancing work with other aspects of life. Rather than viewing work and life as competing priorities, work-life integration creates harmony, allowing individuals to pursue their professional goals while maintaining their well-being and relationships. This approach recognises that productivity is not just about the number of hours worked but also about the quality of those hours and the individual's overall satisfaction.

Another alternative is the concept of "slow work", which challenges the idea that faster is always better. Slow emphasises the importance of taking time to think, reflect, and produce high-quality work rather than rushing to meet deadlines and quotas. This approach is aligned with the principles of "deep work", as articulated by Cal Newport (2016), which advocates for focused, uninterrupted work that allows for creativity and problem-solving. By slowing down and prioritising quality over quantity, individuals can produce more meaningful and impactful work while avoiding burnout. Another critical flaw in the hustle mentality is its disregard for rest and recovery. The idea that sleep is for the weak or that taking breaks is a sign of laziness is not only scientifically inaccurate but also dangerous. Sleep, for instance, is essential for cognitive functioning, emotional regulation, and overall health. Research by Walker (2017) highlights the severe consequences of sleep deprivation, including impaired judgement, increased risk of chronic diseases, and a weakened immune system. Yet, the hustle mentality encourages individuals to sacrifice sleep for productivity, perpetuating a cycle of exhaustion and diminished well-being. The hustle mentality promotes a narrow, individualistic view of success that ignores the broader social and economic factors contributing to inequality. In this worldview, success results from hard work and personal effort, while failure is attributed to a lack of hustle. This narrative conveniently overlooks the structural barriers that many individuals face, such as poverty, discrimination, and lack of access to education and resources. As a result, the hustle mentality can reinforce social inequalities by perpetuating the myth that anyone can succeed if they work hard enough. This ignores the reality that success often depends on factors beyond an individual's control.

The hustle mentality also has implications for mental health. The constant pressure to achieve and the fear of falling behind can lead to anxiety, depression, and a pervasive sense of inadequacy. In a culture that glorifies relentless work, there is little room for vulnerability or failure. Individuals who are struggling are often made to feel as though they are not trying hard enough, leading to feelings of shame and isolation. This toxic cycle is exacerbated by the hustle culture's emphasis on outward success and the constant need to prove oneself to others. Research by Stoeber and Childs (2011) on perfectionism supports this, showing that the relentless pursuit of perfection, often driven by societal expectations, is associated with higher levels of anxiety and depression. The hustle mentality's focus on individual achievement can erode social connections and community. Relationships can become secondary to pursuing goals in a culture that prizes personal success above all else. This can lead to disconnection and loneliness as individuals prioritise work over meaningful social interactions. The emphasis on individualism also undermines the importance of collaboration and collective action. In the workplace, this can create a competitive environment where employees are pitted against each other rather than encouraged to work together. This not only diminishes trust and teamwork but also stifles innovation and creativity.

The notion of "progress" in modern capitalist economies is often heralded by technological advances, increased productivity, and the promise of upward social mobility. Yet, for all these promises, one area where progress has stalled – if not regressed – is in real wages. Over the last 70 years, real wages, when adjusted for inflation, have experienced a relative decline, particularly when compared to the massive gains in productivity. This decline in real wages is not just a mere statistical anomaly; it reflects broader socio-economic shifts, including the weakening of labour unions, globalisation, technological advancements, and the rise of neoliberal economic policies that have fundamentally altered the landscape of work and compensation.

## Meanwhile … Real Term Wage Decline

The period following World War II, often referred to as the "Golden Age of Capitalism", saw substantial wage growth. This era, particularly between the late 1940s and the early 1970s, was marked by strong unions, government policies favouring full employment, and an economic environment where productivity gains translated into higher worker wages. According to the Economic Policy Institute (EPI), from 1948 to 1973, productivity in the United States grew by 96.7%, and real hourly compensation of production and nonsupervisory workers rose by 91.3%, in lockstep (Mishel, Gould, & Bivens, 2015). This close relationship between productivity and wages meant that as companies became more efficient and profitable, the benefits were shared with the workforce. This period represented an egalitarian distribution of wealth, and workers could expect their living standards to rise along with the economy's growth. However, beginning in the mid-1970s, this trend began to unravel. A combination of factors, including the oil crises of the 1970s, the decline of manufacturing jobs, the weakening of labour unions, and the shift towards more service-oriented economies, contributed to the decoupling of productivity and wage growth. While productivity continued to rise, real wages stagnated. Between 1973 and 2013, productivity in the United States increased by 74.4%, yet hourly compensation for production and nonsupervisory workers grew by only 9.2% (Mishel et al., 2015). This divergence points to a significant shift in how the gains from economic growth were distributed.

One of the most significant contributors to the decline in real wages has been the weakening of labour unions. During the post-war period, unions played a crucial role in negotiating better wages, benefits, and working conditions for workers. However, from the 1980s onwards, union membership declined sharply, particularly in the United States and the United Kingdom, where neoliberal policies under leaders like Ronald Reagan and Margaret Thatcher actively sought to undermine union power. According to the Bureau of Labor Statistics (BLS), union membership in the U.S. fell from 20.1% of the workforce in 1983 to just 10.3% in 2021 (BLS, 2021). The decline in union power has weakened workers' bargaining positions, leading to stagnant wages even as companies report record profits and CEO compensation soars. Globalisation has also played a critical role in the decline of real wages. The integration of global markets has led to offshoring manufacturing jobs to countries with lower labour costs, which has exerted downward pressure on wages in developed countries. As companies have moved production overseas, workers in higher-wage countries have faced job losses and wage cuts. Moreover, the threat of offshoring has been used as leverage against workers' demands for higher wages. A study by Autor, Dorn, and Hanson (2013) found that regions in the United States exposed to competition from Chinese imports experienced significant declines in manufacturing employment and wages.

Technological advancements, while driving productivity, have also contributed to wage stagnation and inequality. Automation and the rise of information technology have disproportionately benefited high-skilled workers, leading to wage polarisation. While workers in highly skilled jobs have seen wage increases, those in low-skilled, routine jobs have faced stagnant or declining wages. Technology's displacement of middle-wage jobs has hollowed out the labour market, leaving many workers in low-wage service jobs with limited opportunities for upward mobility. Neoliberal economic policies prioritising deregulation, privatisation, and free-market principles have further exacerbated the decline in real wages. These policies have often been accompanied by tax cuts for the wealthy, reductions in social safety nets, and a push for labour market flexibility, all of which have eroded workers' bargaining power and income security. The shift from a manufacturing-based economy to a service-based one has also played a role, as service sector jobs tend to pay lower wages and offer fewer benefits than manufacturing jobs. The rise of gig and precarious work, where workers lack the stability and protections of traditional employment, has further contributed to wage stagnation and inequality.

The consequences of declining real wages are profound. For one, they have led to increased income inequality, as the benefits of economic growth have increasingly flowed to the top of the income distribution. According to the World Inequality Report 2022, the share of income held by the top 1% of earners in the United States increased from 11% in 1980 to 20% in 2021 (Chancel et al., 2022). This growing inequality has far-reaching implications for social cohesion, political stability, and economic growth. As wealth concentrates at the top, the middle and working classes struggle to maintain their standard of living, leading to increased debt, financial insecurity, and social unrest. The decline in real wages significantly affects consumer demand and economic growth. In a consumer-driven economy, stagnant wages mean less disposable income for households to spend on goods and services, leading to slower economic growth. This dynamic is particularly concerning in the context of rising living costs, including housing, healthcare, and education, which have outpaced wage growth. The result is a growing gap between the cost of living and workers' ability to afford necessities, leading to increased reliance on credit and a precarious financial situation for many households. In response to these challenges, there has been growing debate about the need for policy interventions to address wage stagnation and inequality. Instead of a mindless hustle mentality, proposals include raising the minimum wage, strengthening labour rights and protections, investing in education and training to help workers adapt to technological change, and implementing progressive tax policies to redistribute wealth. Additionally, there is a growing recognition of the need for a more comprehensive approach to measuring economic well-being beyond GDP and productivity that considers factors such as income distribution, job quality, and access to essential services.

## A Dilemma of Modern Society

*Into the Wild* (2007), directed by Sean Penn and based on Jon Krakauer's nonfiction book, tells the story of Christopher McCandless, a young man disillusioned with society and the trappings of modern life who ventures into the Alaskan wilderness in search of a purer, more authentic existence. McCandless's journey seems like the ultimate act of self-help: a bold rejection of societal norms to pursue personal freedom and self-actualisation. But beneath the surface, *Into the Wild* is a story about toxic positivity and individualism. Emile Hirsch's earnest portrayal of McCandless embodies the archetype of the self-reliant individual who believes that happiness and fulfilment lie in escaping the constraints of society. He donates his savings to charity, abandons his family, and sets out on a solitary journey across America, aiming to live off the land in the remote wilderness of Alaska. His idealism and determination are admirable but also concerning, reflecting the relentless positivity that often permeates self-help narratives. At its core, toxic positivity is the belief that maintaining an unwaveringly positive attitude is the key to overcoming any obstacle. It dismisses the complexity of human emotions and experiences, reducing them to simplistic notions of "good vibes only" and "mind over matter". McCandless's journey is, in many ways, an embodiment of this mindset. He approaches his quest with relentless optimism, convinced that he can achieve true freedom and happiness by shedding the burdens of modern life. However, this optimism closes his eyes to the realities of his situation and the limitations of his abilities.

One of the most striking aspects of *Into the Wild* is how it subtly critiques the ideas that drive McCandless. The film does not shy away from showing the consequences of his idealism. As McCandless ventures deeper into the wilderness, his romantic notions of self-sufficiency crumble. The Alaskan landscape, while breathtakingly beautiful, is also harsh and unforgiving. McCandless's lack of preparation and experience becomes painfully apparent as he struggles to find food, shelter, and warmth. His toxic positivity, the belief that he can overcome any challenge through sheer willpower, leads him to ignore the dangers he faces. In this sense, *Into the Wild* can be seen as a critique of the self-help industry's often unrealistic promises. Just as McCandless believes escaping society will bring him happiness, self-help books frequently peddle the idea that success and fulfilment are simply a matter of adopting the right mindset. They encourage readers to believe they can achieve anything if they think positively, work hard, and ignore the naysayers (critical friends). But this message is not only misleading; it can also be dangerous. It promotes a kind of magical thinking that disregards the complexities of life and the external factors that often shape our experiences. McCandless's journey highlights the pitfalls of extreme individualism. His desire to live apart from family, community and society is rooted in rejecting the interconnectedness that defines human existence. In his quest for solitude, McCandless isolates himself from the very people who care about him – his family, friends, and the kind strangers he meets. This isolation, while initially empowering, becomes his undoing. Alone in the wilderness, he has no one to turn to for help when things go wrong.

This aspect of the film resonates with the critique of individualism that runs through much of the self-help literature. While important, the emphasis on self-reliance and personal responsibility can also lead to a sense of disconnection from others. It creates the belief that we are solely responsible for our success or failure, ignoring the role that community, supporting networks, friends and social structures play in shaping our lives. McCandless's end is a reminder that no one is self-sufficient and that rejecting community bonds can have detrimental consequences. Yet, *Into the Wild* does not entirely condemn McCandless's quest. The film captures the beauty and allure of the natural world, the sense of wonder and freedom that comes from stepping outside the boundaries of society. It acknowledges the appeal of the self-help narrative – the desire to take control of one's life, to break free from the pressures and expectations of the world, and to seek out a more authentic existence. However, it also urges viewers to recognise the limits of this approach. In the film's final moments, McCandless comes to a profound realisation: "Happiness is only real when shared." This simple truth encapsulates the film's ultimate message. While pursuing personal growth and self-discovery is valuable, it cannot be separated from our relationships with others. Fulfilment comes not from isolation but through connection – the bonds we form with those around us, the communities we are part of, and the shared experiences that enrich our lives.

*Into the Wild* offers a powerful critique of toxic positivity and the dangers of glorifying individualism at the expense of the community. It challenges the simplistic narratives in self-help culture, reminding us that life is complex, unpredictable, and often beyond our control. In the end, McCandless's story is a cautionary narrative about the limits of self-reliance and the importance of recognising our need for connection and support. As we navigate the pressures of modern life, it is tempting to believe that we can overcome any obstacle through positive thinking and sheer determination. But *Into the Wild* reminds us there is no shame in acknowledging our limitations, seeking help, and finding strength in our relationships. True happiness and fulfilment are not found in the pursuit of perfection or the rejection of society. Still, we share with those around us in the messy, imperfect, and interconnected world.

Modern society's balance between individualism and community has become one of the most contentious ideological battlegrounds. The cultural, economic, and political landscape of the twenty-first century has increasingly tilted towards individualism, often at the expense of community. This shift has profound implications for social cohesion, mental health, and the broader fabric of society. I argue that the overemphasis on individualism – while fostering innovation and personal freedom – can undermine the communal bonds that sustain us. This discussion aims to critically examine the dominance of individualism over community in modern society, drawing on empirical evidence, scholarly research, and contemporary examples to illuminate the consequences of this ideological imbalance.

The roots of individualism can be traced back to the Enlightenment, a period in the seventeenth and eighteenth centuries when thinkers such as John Locke and Jean-Jacques Rousseau championed the rights and autonomy of the individual. These ideas laid the groundwork for modern liberal democracies, where protecting individual rights and freedoms is paramount. However, the Enlightenment's celebration of the individual was not meant to negate the importance of community; rather, it was intended to empower individuals within the context of a broader social contract (Rousseau, 1762). The problem arises when this balance is disrupted, and individualism becomes an end rather than a means to achieve a more just and equitable society.

In contemporary societies, particularly Western societies, the ideology of individualism has reached new heights. The neoliberal economic model, which has dominated global politics since the late twentieth century, strongly emphasises individual responsibility, self-reliance, and personal achievement. This model is predicated on the belief that the free market, driven by self-interested individuals, is the most efficient and just way to allocate resources and opportunities (Harvey, 2005). The rise of neoliberalism has been accompanied by a corresponding decline in the state's role in providing social welfare, with individuals increasingly expected to fend for themselves in a competitive marketplace.

This shift towards individualism has been lauded for promoting innovation, entrepreneurship, and economic growth. Individualism has undoubtedly contributed to technological advancements, medicine, and industry by incentivising personal achievement and rewarding those who take risks. However, the relentless focus on individual success comes at a cost. As sociologist Robert Putnam (2000) famously argued in *Bowling Alone*, the rise of individualism has led to a decline in social capital – the networks, norms, and trust that enable people to work together for mutual benefit. Putnam's research shows that Americans are becoming increasingly disconnected from their communities, with fewer people participating in civic activities, joining clubs, or spending time with friends and neighbours.

The decline in social capital is not just a quaint observation about changing social habits; it has severe implications for public health and well-being. Research has consistently shown that strong social connections are crucial for mental and physical health. A study by Holt-Lunstad, Smith, and Layton (2010) found that individuals with strong social relationships have a 50% higher likelihood of survival than those with weaker social ties. This finding underscores the importance of community and social support in promoting longevity. Yet, the dominance of individualism in modern society often leads to social isolation, loneliness, and a breakdown of the essential communal bonds for well-being.

The mental health crisis that has emerged in recent years can be partially attributed to the prioritisation of individualism over community. The pressure to succeed and the stigma associated with asking for help can lead to feelings of inadequacy and isolation. The rise of social media, while connecting people, has paradoxically exacerbated this problem by creating a culture of comparison and competition. Individuals are constantly bombarded with images of others' curated successes, leading to a pervasive sense of "not measuring up". The result is a society where people are increasingly isolated, anxious, and depressed despite being more "connected" than ever before (Twenge, 2017). The focus on individualism undermines collective action and the pursuit of the common good. In a society where personal success is prioritised, there is less incentive to engage in activities that benefit the community but may not directly reward the individual. This can lead to declining civic engagement and participation in democratic processes. For example, voter turnout in many Western democracies has steadily declined, particularly among younger generations who may feel disillusioned by a political system that seems disconnected from their needs and concerns (Putnam, 2000). The emphasis on individualism also makes it more challenging to address systemic issues such as poverty, inequality, and climate change, which require collective action and a willingness to put the common good above personal gain.

The impact of individualism on economic inequality is particularly stark. While individualism promotes the idea that anyone can succeed if they work hard enough, this narrative often obscures the structural barriers that prevent many people from achieving their full potential. Economic inequality has increased in many countries, with the gap between the rich and the poor widening significantly over the past few decades (Piketty, 2014). The emphasis on individual responsibility has led to policies favouring the wealthy and well-connected, while social safety nets and public services that benefit the broader community have been eroded. The result is a society where the benefits of economic growth are increasingly concentrated in the hands of a few while the majority struggle to make ends meet. Glorifying individualism can lead to moral relativism, where personal success is seen as the goal, regardless of the impact on others. This mentality is evident in the rise of hustle culture, where overwork and burnout are celebrated as badges of honour, and in the cutthroat competitiveness of specific industries where ethics and empathy are often sacrificed in the name of profit. The emphasis on individual achievement can also lead to a lack of empathy for those less fortunate, as their struggles are often dismissed as the result of personal failings rather than systemic issues.

The dominance of individualism over community also has implications for environmental sustainability. The consumerist culture that has emerged alongside individualism encourages people to define themselves by what they own, leading to overconsumption and ecological degradation. Focusing on personal success and material wealth often comes at the planet's expense, as natural resources are exploited to fuel economic growth. Addressing environmental challenges such as climate change requires a shift from individualism to a more collective mindset that prioritises the well-being of the community and future generations (Klein, 2014). Considering these issues, it is clear that overemphasising individualism at the expense of community is a significant problem in modern society. While individualism has its merits, particularly in promoting personal freedom and innovation, it must be balanced with recognising the importance of community, social support, and the common good. To address the challenges posed by the dominance of individualism, we need to foster a culture that values collaboration, empathy, and collective action.

One way to achieve this balance is through education. Schools and universities have a crucial role in teaching students not just the skills they need to succeed as individuals but also the importance of contributing to the well-being of their communities. Civic education, community service, and collaborative learning experiences can help students develop a sense of social responsibility and a commitment to the common good. By emphasising the value of community alongside individual achievement, we can help to create a more balanced and equitable society. Another critical step is strengthening social safety nets and public services supporting the community. This includes investing in healthcare, education, housing, and social services that ensure everyone can succeed, regardless of their background or circumstances. By prioritising the community's well-being, we can help reduce inequality and create a society where everyone has the chance to thrive. We must challenge cultural narratives glorifying individualism and promote a more balanced view of success. This means recognising that personal achievement is not the only measure of a meaningful life and that our well-being is deeply interconnected with the well-being of others. By advocating a culture that values empathy, cooperation, and the common good, we can create a more resilient, equitable, and sustainable society.

# Chapter 5

# How Self-Help Shifts Blame
# onto the Individual

Self-help has emerged as a dominant force, promising individuals the tools to transform their lives, achieve success, and find happiness. With its roots in positive thinking and personal empowerment, this genre has grown into a multi-billion-dollar industry catering to an audience hungry for success. However, beneath the motivational rhetoric lies a more insidious aspect of self-help – its tendency to shift blame onto the individual for their struggles and failures. Self-help offers a sense of agency in an overwhelming and chaotic global situation. By following the advice of self-help gurus, individuals believe they can take control of their destinies and overcome any obstacle in their path. This narrative is deeply rooted in the American Dream, which posits that hard work, determination, and a positive attitude are all that is needed to succeed. However, this focus on individual effort comes at a cost. By emphasising personal responsibility, self-help often fails to acknowledge the systemic barriers preventing individuals from achieving their goals. This omission is not merely a flaw in the self-help narrative but a fundamental aspect of its appeal.

The self-help industry promises personal transformation and empowerment. Still, it perpetuates a culture of self-obsession, superficiality and individualism, concerns noted by Christopher Lasch in his *The Culture of Narcissism* (1979), where he argues that the rise of narcissism in American culture reflects a broader societal shift towards self-absorption and away from community and collective well-being. He argued that the post-World War II era brought about significant shifts in American society, leading to a decline in traditional values such as community, family, and civic responsibility, which were replaced with a new preoccupation with the self, personal fulfilment, and individual success. Lasch described this shift as the rise of a "culture of narcissism" where people became increasingly focused on their own needs, desires, and self-image at the expense of broader social and communal concerns. Lasch's critique was rooted in psychoanalytic theory, particularly the work of Sigmund Freud and his followers, who explored the concept of narcissism as a psychological disorder. However, Lasch extended the idea of narcissism beyond individual pathology to describe a broader cultural phenomenon. He argued that various societal changes, including the decline of traditional institutions, the rise of consumer capitalism, and the proliferation of mass media, fuelled the culture of narcissism. These forces, Lasch contended, created a society in which individuals were encouraged to prioritise their self-interest, pursue material success, and cultivate a carefully curated public persona (seen today through social media). Fast forward to the present day, and the self-help industry is both a product and a perpetrator of the culture of narcissism that Lasch described. The industry can be traced back to the same societal forces that Lasch identified, particularly the increasing emphasis on individualism and the commodification of personal success. In many ways, the self-help industry has capitalised on the cultural shift towards narcissism by offering individuals the tools and strategies to achieve their personal goals, often with little regard for the broader social context.

One of the most significant ways in which the self-help industry perpetuates a culture of narcissism is through its relentless focus on the self. Self-help books, seminars, and online courses often emphasise the importance of self-empowerment, self-actualisation, and self-improvement. The self is undergoing constant DIY. While these concepts may seem optimistic, they usually encourage a narrow, individualistic approach to personal growth that overlooks the importance of community, relationships, and social responsibility. In this sense, the self-help industry reinforces the notion that personal success is the goal and that individuals are solely responsible for their happiness and well-being. The self-help industry often promotes a superficial understanding of personal growth, primarily concerned with outward appearances and material success. This is evident in the proliferation of books and programmes that promise to help individuals achieve financial prosperity, physical attractiveness, and social status. Such messages are closely aligned with the narcissistic values that Lasch critiqued, which prioritise image, status, and material wealth over deeper, more meaningful forms of fulfilment. In this context, the self-help industry can be seen as a continuation of the culture of narcissism, encouraging individuals to focus on their self-interest and to measure their worth in terms of external achievements.

Lasch's critique that resonates with today's self-help industry focuses on the illusion of control. Lasch argued that the culture of narcissism was characterised by a desire for control, both over oneself and one's environment. This desire for control is evident in the self-help industry's emphasis on personal agency and the belief that individuals can shape their destinies through sheer willpower and positive thinking. Self-help gurus often espouse the idea that anyone can achieve their dreams if they are willing to put in the effort, adopt the right mindset, and follow the prescribed steps. Lasch also critiqued the commodification of the self, a process that has only intensified in the decades since his book was published. In today's self-help industry, personal development has become a commodity. This commodification reflects the broader trend of consumer culture, where everything, including personal growth, is transformed into a product to be marketed. The commodification of the self is closely tied to the culture of narcissism, as it encourages individuals to view themselves as projects to be managed and optimised. This mindset is evident in the self-help industry's emphasis on self-improvement as a lifelong endeavour that requires constant investment in new tools, strategies, and products. The result is a cycle of consumption, where individuals are encouraged to seek new ways to improve themselves continually. One of the most significant consequences of the culture of narcissism is the erosion of community and collective responsibility. In a society prioritising individual success and self-interest, the bonds that hold communities together are weakened, and the sense of collective responsibility is diminished. This erosion of community is evident in the self-help industry's focus on individual transformation, often at the expense of social and communal concerns. Many self-help programmes emphasise the importance of setting personal goals and achieving individual success. Still, they rarely address the broader social and environmental factors that shape individuals' lives. This narrow focus on the self can lead to isolation, as individuals are encouraged to prioritise their needs and desires over those of their community. In this context, the self-help industry can be seen as contributing to the decline of social cohesion and the weakening of the social fabric that Lasch warned about. Lasch also identified a paradox at the heart of the culture of narcissism: the more individuals focus on themselves and their success, the more insecure and anxious they become. This paradox is evident in today's self-help industry, where the relentless pursuit of self-improvement can lead to feelings of inadequacy, anxiety, and self-doubt. Despite the industry's promises of empowerment and personal transformation, many individuals are trapped in constant self-evaluation and self-criticism.

One of the most significant ways in which self-help shifts blame onto the individual is by promoting the idea that success is solely a matter of mindset. Books suggest that positive thinking and visualisation are the keys to wealth, health, and happiness. These books imply that if individuals are not successful, they are not thinking positively enough or visualising their goals sufficiently. This narrative places the burden of success squarely on the individual, ignoring the social, economic, and structural factors that can impede progress. For example, someone living in poverty may be unable to afford the education or resources needed to achieve their goals, no matter how positively they think. By focusing on mindset, self-help obscures these barriers and reinforces the notion that failure is a personal failing rather than a consequence of broader social inequities. The emphasis on personal responsibility in self-help can lead to feelings of shame and inadequacy when individuals cannot achieve the desired outcomes. The narrative that "you are the master of your destiny" can be empowering when things are going well, but it can also be devastating when life takes an unexpected turn. For instance, someone who loses their job due to an economic downturn or who struggles with mental health issues may internalise the belief that they are to blame for their circumstances. This internalisation can lead to a vicious cycle of self-blame, where individuals feel increasingly powerless and overwhelmed by their perceived failures. Instead of seeking support or recognising the external factors contributing to their struggles, they may retreat further into themselves, believing they must "fix" their mindset before changing their situation.

The self-help industry's focus on individualism also perpetuates a narrow definition of success, often rooted in material wealth and social status. Many self-help books equate success with financial prosperity, career advancement, and personal achievement. This definition is limiting and exclusionary, as it fails to recognise the diversity of human experience and how people find meaning and fulfilment in their lives. For example, someone who values community, relationships, or creativity over material success may feel alienated by the self-help narrative, which often equates personal worth with financial success. This narrow focus on individual

101

achievement can also reinforce harmful stereotypes about less successful people, implying that they are lazy, unmotivated, or lacking in ambition. The self-help industry often overlooks the role of systemic oppression in shaping individuals' lives. Issues such as racism, sexism, ableism, and classism are rarely addressed in self-help literature, which tends to focus on the individual's ability to overcome obstacles through sheer willpower. This omission is particularly problematic because it reinforces the idea that individuals are solely responsible for their success or failure, ignoring how systemic oppression can create significant barriers to achievement. For example, a woman of colour may face discrimination in the workplace that limits her opportunities for advancement, no matter how hard she works or how positively she thinks. By failing to acknowledge these barriers, self-help perpetuates the myth of meritocracy – the idea that everyone has an equal opportunity to succeed if they work hard – while ignoring systemic inequality's reality (Littler, 2018).

The consequences of this individualistic focus are not limited to the personal level. By promoting the idea that success is solely a matter of personal responsibility, self-help can also undermine collective action and social change. When individuals are led to believe that they are entirely responsible for their circumstances, they may be less likely to recognise the need for systemic change or to engage in collective efforts to address social issues. This shift in focus from the collective to the individual is not accidental – it is deeply rooted in the neoliberal ideology that underpins much of the self-help industry (Illouz, 2008). Neoliberalism, emphasising free markets, individualism, and personal responsibility, has shaped the self-help industry's narrative, promoting the idea that individuals should solve their problems rather than relying on the state or other forms of collective support (Harvey, 2005). This focus on individualism can also have broader societal implications. When people are encouraged to view their success or failure as entirely within their control, they may be less likely to support policies that address social inequality or help those in need. For example, suppose someone believes that poverty results from laziness or lack of motivation. In that case, they may be less likely to support policies that provide social safety nets or address economic inequality. This shift in focus from the collective to the individual can undermine efforts to create a more just and equitable society, as it promotes the idea that individuals should be responsible for their well-being, regardless of the systemic factors that may be shaping their lives.

The self-help industry's emphasis on personal responsibility also raises ethical concerns. By shifting the blame onto the individual, self-help can exploit people's vulnerabilities and insecurities, leading them to invest time, money, and energy into products and services that may not address their underlying needs. The industry's focus on quick fixes and simple solutions can also lead to a cycle of dependency, where individuals continually seek out new self-help products to achieve the desired outcomes. This cycle can be emotionally and financially draining as individuals invest in methods that may not be effective or sustainable. Moreover, the lack of regulation in the self-help industry means that consumers are often exposed to dubious claims and unproven methods, with little recourse if these methods fail (Rosen, Glasgow, & Moore, 2003). The self-help industry's focus on individualism and personal responsibility can also have psychological consequences. The pressure to succeed and the belief that failure is a personal failure can lead to increased stress, anxiety, and depression. This is particularly true for individuals already struggling with mental health issues, who may feel overwhelmed by the demands of self-improvement and the expectation to achieve success through sheer willpower. The emphasis on personal responsibility can also discourage individuals from seeking professional help, as they may feel they should be able to solve their problems independently. This reluctance to seek help can delay or prevent recovery, leading to a worsening of symptoms and a greater sense of isolation (Tavris, 2014). The self-help industry's focus on individualism and personal responsibility also reflects broader societal trends, particularly the rise of neoliberalism and the decline of social solidarity. In a neoliberal society, individuals are encouraged to view themselves as entrepreneurs of their lives, responsible for managing their well-being, success, and happiness. A decline in social safety nets has accompanied this shift in focus from the collective to the individual, the erosion of workers' rights, and the dismantling of public services (Harvey, 2005). The self-help industry, with its emphasis on personal empowerment and individual success, has promoted this ideology, encouraging individuals to view their success or failure as a matter of personal responsibility rather than a reflection of broader social and economic forces.

## Blaming the Victim and Responsibilisation

Blaming the victim and responsibilisation have been woven into our cultural, political, and economic narratives. Though seemingly innocuous, these concepts carry significant implications for understanding and addressing social issues. The tendency to blame individuals for their misfortunes and to hold them solely responsible for overcoming systemic challenges reflects a broader ideological shift towards individualism and neoliberalism. This chapter critically examines the pervasive practice of victim blaming and the process of responsibilisation, exploring their roots and consequences, and how they reinforce existing power structures and perpetuate social inequalities. To begin with, the concept of blaming the victim is not new. It has long been a strategy employed to deflect attention from the systemic causes of social problems by attributing responsibility to the individuals suffering from them. The term itself was popularised by William Ryan (2010), who argued that the focus on individual behaviour and personal responsibility often obscures the structural factors contributing to poverty, inequality, and social injustice. According to Ryan, blaming the victim allows society to maintain the status quo by shifting the burden of change onto those least equipped to effect it.

Victim blaming can take many forms, from subtle insinuations to overt accusations. It is often seen in the rhetoric surrounding poverty, where the poor are frequently portrayed as lazy, unmotivated, or lacking in moral character. This narrative suggests that poverty results from personal failings rather than systemic factors such as wage stagnation, unemployment, or lack of access to education and healthcare. For example, the idea that poor people need to work harder or manage their finances better ignores the structural barriers that make it difficult for many to escape poverty, such as the high cost of living, lack of affordable housing, and the decline of well-paying jobs (Gans, 1995). This narrative not only stigmatises people living in poverty but also absolves society of the responsibility to address the root causes of poverty.

Victim blaming is also prevalent in discussions of sexual violence, where survivors are often questioned about their behaviour, clothing, or level of intoxication. The implication is that the victim's actions somehow provoked the assault, thereby shifting responsibility away from the perpetrator. By focusing on the victim's behaviour, society can maintain the illusion that the world is just and that bad things only happen to those who "deserve" it. This belief in a just world, while comforting, serves to perpetuate injustice by minimising the experiences of victims and shielding perpetrators from accountability (Hafer and Sutton, 2016). The process of responsibilisation, closely related to victim blaming, refers to the practice of shifting responsibility for social problems from the state or society to the individual. This concept is rooted in neoliberal ideology, which emphasises individualism, self-reliance, and personal responsibility while downplaying the role of collective action and state intervention. Responsibilisation encourages individuals to view themselves as entrepreneurs of their lives, responsible for managing their health, wealth, and happiness. This shift in focus from the collective to the individual has profound implications for addressing social issues, as it often leads to the privatisation of risk and the erosion of social safety nets (Barry, Osborne and Rose, 2013).

One of the most significant examples of responsibilisation can be seen in healthcare, particularly in public health campaigns emphasising lifestyle changes as the primary means of preventing disease. While promoting healthy behaviours is undoubtedly important, the focus on individual responsibility often obscures the structural determinants of health, such as access to healthcare, socioeconomic status, and environmental factors. For instance, the emphasis on diet and exercise to prevent obesity often fails to acknowledge the role of food deserts, the lack of safe spaces for physical activity, and the impact of poverty on health outcomes (Guthman, 2011). By placing the burden of health solely on the individual, responsibilisation diverts attention from the need for systemic changes to address these underlying issues. The responsibilisation of health is also evident in the rise of wellness culture, where individuals are encouraged to take control of their health through mindfulness, yoga, and clean eating practices. While these practices can contribute to well-being, they are often framed as personal choices that are entirely within the individual's control. This narrative ignores how structural factors, such as income inequality, lack of access to healthcare, and social isolation, can impact health and well-being. Moreover, the commercialisation of wellness culture often leads to the commodification of health, where individuals are encouraged to purchase products and services that promise to enhance their well-being (Cederström & Spicer, 2015). This commodification reinforces the idea that health is a personal responsibility and exacerbates social inequalities by making wellness accessible only to those who can afford it.

Responsibilisation is also a key feature of neoliberal labour markets, where workers are increasingly expected to take responsibility for their employment outcomes. The rise of the gig economy, characterised by precarious work, lack of job security, and the erosion of traditional labour protections, is a prime example of this trend. Workers are encouraged to view themselves as independent contractors or entrepreneurs responsible for managing their careers and financial security. This shift in responsibility has significant implications for workers' rights, as it often leads to the erosion of collective bargaining power, the weakening of labour protections, and the dismantling of social safety nets (Standing, 2015). By framing work as a matter of individual responsibility, neoliberal labour markets effectively absolve employers and the state of the responsibility to provide secure, well-paying jobs and protect workers from exploitation. The consequences of responsibilisation extend beyond the individual to the broader social and political landscape. By shifting responsibility onto individuals, responsibilisation undermines the social contract, which holds that the state should protect the well-being of its citizens. This erosion of the social contract can lead to the dismantling of social safety nets, the privatisation of public services, and the weakening of regulatory frameworks that protect citizens from harm. In this context, individuals are left to navigate increasingly precarious social and economic environments with little support from the state or society. The result is a society where social inequalities are exacerbated, and the most vulnerable are left to face systemic failures.

The process of responsibilisation also has significant implications for social justice and collective action. By emphasising individual responsibility, responsibilisation discourages collective action and undermines the potential for social movements to address systemic issues. When individuals are led to believe that their success or failure is solely a matter of personal effort, they may be less likely to recognise the structural barriers that impede their progress and less likely to engage in collective efforts to address these barriers. This shift in focus from the collective to the individual weakens social solidarity. It reinforces existing power structures, making it more difficult to challenge the status quo and effect meaningful change (Brown, 2015). The emphasis on personal responsibility in responsibilisation can lead to the internalisation of blame and the pathologisation of individuals who cannot meet societal expectations. This internalisation can have significant psychological consequences, leading to feelings of shame, guilt, and inadequacy. For example, individuals unable to find stable employment or achieve financial security may internalise the belief that they are to blame for their circumstances, leading to a sense of failure and hopelessness. This internalisation can also stigmatise those unable to meet societal expectations, reinforcing social hierarchies and perpetuating inequality (Wacquant and Wacquant, 2020).

The intersection of victim blaming and responsibilisation is particularly evident in the context of welfare policy, where individuals who rely on social assistance are often portrayed as morally deficient or lacking in personal responsibility. The rhetoric surrounding welfare reform usually emphasises the need to incentivise work and reduce dependency on state support, framing welfare recipients as passive or lazy individuals who need to be "activated" or "disciplined" into becoming productive members of society (Peck, 2001). This narrative not only stigmatises welfare recipients but also obscures the structural factors that contribute to poverty and unemployment, such as the decline of well-paying jobs, the rise of precarious work, and the erosion of labour protections. By framing welfare as a matter of personal responsibility, policymakers can justify cuts to social assistance programmes and the implementation of punitive measures, such as work requirements and time limits, that further entrench poverty and inequality. The implications of victim blaming and responsibilisation extend beyond welfare policy to other areas of social policy, including criminal justice, education, and housing.

The emphasis on personal responsibility is evident in the rhetoric surrounding academic achievement and school reform. Students who fail to meet academic standards are often blamed for their lack of effort or motivation, with little attention paid to the structural factors that impact educational outcomes, such as funding disparities, racial segregation, and the impact of poverty on learning. This narrative stigmatises students who struggle academically and undermines efforts to address the systemic inequalities contributing to educational disparities (Ladson-Billings, 2006). In housing, the responsibilisation of individuals is evident in the shift towards market-based solutions to housing affordability, where individuals are encouraged to take responsibility for their own housing needs through homeownership or participation in the private rental market. This shift in responsibility has significant implications for housing policy, as it often leads to the erosion of public housing and the commodification of housing as a market good rather than a social right. The result is a housing market that increasingly serves the interests of investors and developers rather than the needs of low-income and marginalised communities (Aalbers, 2016).

Best-selling authors, motivational speakers, and self-proclaimed gurus flood the market with tales of triumph – of lives transformed, fortunes made, and happiness attained.

These narratives are potent; they captivate our imaginations, tug at our aspirations, and offer a glimmer of hope that we, too, might unlock the secrets to a better life. Yet, for every success story, countless others tell a tale that remains untold mainly – stories of self-help failures, shattered expectations, and the emotional toll of these unmet promises. It is important to explore these narratives, understand the nebulous side of the self-help phenomenon, and explore the profound psychological impact these failures can have on individuals. At the heart of the self-help industry lies a paradox. It is an industry built on personal empowerment, promising that anyone can achieve their goals with the right mindset, tools, and strategies. Yet, this promise often comes with an unspoken caveat: failure reflects personal inadequacy. When individuals invest time, money, and emotional energy into self-help programmes, only to find that their lives remain unchanged or even worsened, the blame is frequently turned inward. This internalisation of failure can lead to a range of adverse psychological outcomes, including anxiety, depression, and a diminished sense of self-worth.

Consider the story of Sarah, a 35-year-old woman who turned to self-help books after experiencing personal and professional setbacks. Like many others, Sarah was drawn to the self-help genre by its seductive promise of control – control over her emotions, career, and relationships. She devoured books on positive thinking, mindfulness, and goal setting, each promising that change was within her grasp if only she would follow the prescribed steps. Yet, despite her best efforts, Sarah was stuck in the same behaviour patterns, her life stubbornly refusing to conform to the optimistic narratives she had been fed. The result was a profound sense of failure and frustration. Instead of feeling empowered, Sarah felt more lost than ever, her faith in herself eroded by the tools that were supposed to help her. Sarah's story is far from unique. Research has shown that self-help interventions can benefit some but are not a panacea. A study by Rosen, Glasgow, and Moore (2003) found that self-help materials are often no more effective than a placebo, and in some cases, they can even be harmful. The problem lies not only in the content of these materials but in how they are marketed. Self-help books and programmes are often sold as quick fixes, with catchy titles and step-by-step guides that promise rapid results. This creates unrealistic expectations, leading individuals to believe that they should be able to achieve significant change with minimal effort. When these expectations are not met, the resulting disappointment can be crushing.

The emotional toll of self-help failures is further compounded by the pervasive personal responsibility narrative underpinning the industry. The self-help genre is deeply rooted in neoliberal ideology, emphasising individualism, self-reliance, and personal responsibility. This ideology is reflected in the rhetoric of self-help books, which often suggest that individuals are solely responsible for their success or failure. While this message can be empowering for some, it can also be deeply damaging for others, particularly those who are already struggling with feelings of inadequacy or low self-esteem. When individuals fail to achieve the outcomes promised by self-help materials, they may internalise this failure as a reflection of their worth, leading to shame, guilt, and self-blame (Illouz, 2008).

The emotional toll of self-help failures is not limited to feelings of personal inadequacy. It can also lead to a sense of isolation and disconnection. The self-help industry often promotes a narrative of individualism, encouraging people to look inward for solutions to their problems. This inward focus can lead to self-absorption that alienates individuals from their social support networks, leaving them to grapple with their struggles alone. Moreover, the emphasis on personal responsibility can discourage individuals from seeking help from others, whether through therapy, community support, or social activism. This isolation can exacerbate mental health issues, leading to a vicious cycle of failure and self-blame.

Let's imagine John, a 42-year-old man who turned to self-help after a series of failed business ventures, to illustrate this point. John was drawn to books on entrepreneurship and financial success, each promising that he could turn his fortunes around with the right mindset and strategies. He invested heavily in these materials, attended seminars and bought into expensive coaching programmes. Yet, despite his efforts, his businesses continued to fail. As his financial situation worsened, John found himself withdrawing from friends and family, ashamed to admit that he had not been able to achieve the success that he had been promised. The result was a deep sense of loneliness and despair as John became increasingly isolated and disconnected from the very people who could have offered him support.

John's experience highlights another critical issue with the self-help industry: its failure to account for structural and systemic factors contributing to individual struggles. The self-help genre often promotes the idea that success is purely a matter of personal effort, ignoring the broader social, economic, and political contexts in which people live. This narrative can be particularly harmful to individuals from marginalised or disadvantaged backgrounds, who may face significant barriers to success that are beyond their control. When these individuals fail to achieve the outcomes promised by self-help materials, they may feel inadequate and disillusioned with the entire self-help enterprise.

This disconnect between the promises of self-help and the reality of life is particularly evident in the stories of those who have experienced significant trauma or adversity. For these individuals, the simplistic solutions offered by self-help books can feel inadequate and dismissive of their lived experiences. The emphasis on positive thinking and personal responsibility can invalidate the genuine pain and suffering these individuals have endured, leading to anger, resentment, and betrayal. This is especially true for those who have turned to self-help as a last resort, hoping to find solace and guidance in their darkest moments, only to be met with empty platitudes and unrealistic expectations. The emotional toll of self-help failures is increased by the lack of accountability within the industry. Unlike other forms of psychological intervention, self-help materials are not subject to the same rigorous standards of evidence and efficacy. This lack of oversight means that individuals are often left to navigate the self-help landscape independently, with little guidance on what works and what does not. The result is a marketplace flooded with dubious claims and unproven techniques, leaving consumers vulnerable to exploitation and harm (Tavris, 2014). The lack of regulation also means that there is little recourse for those harmed by self-help materials, further compounding the emotional toll of failure. The self-help industry, a multi-billion-dollar enterprise, thrives on the promise of personal transformation. From books and seminars to online courses and motivational speeches, the central narrative of self-help is simple yet powerful: individual effort, mindset, and perseverance are the keys to success and happiness. This seductive narrative offers a sense of control in an often chaotic and unpredictable world.

The self-help genre's emphasis on individualism is rooted in the broader cultural context of neoliberalism, a political and economic ideology that has dominated much of the Western world since the late twentieth century. Neoliberalism promotes free markets, deregulation, and minimal government intervention, emphasising that individuals are responsible for their success or failure. This ideology is reflected in the self-help industry, which often portrays personal problems as the result of individual failings rather than systemic issues, for example, books encouraging readers to focus on their thoughts, attitudes, and behaviours as the primary determinants of their circumstances. While there is value in cultivating a positive mindset and taking personal responsibility for one's actions, the self-help industry's narrow focus on individualism often overlooks the web of external factors that influence our lives. For example, consider the issue of poverty. Self-help books frequently suggest that financial success is simply a matter of adopting the right mindset, setting goals, and working hard. However, this perspective ignores the structural factors that contribute to poverty, such as lack of access to quality education, systemic racism, and economic inequality. These are not issues that can be overcome through positive thinking alone; they require collective action and systemic change.

The self-help industry's tendency to ignore external factors is particularly evident in its treatment of mental health. Many self-help books promote the idea that mental health issues can be resolved through individual efforts, such as practising mindfulness, changing negative thought patterns, or adopting a more positive attitude. While these strategies can be helpful, they are often presented as stand-alone solutions without consideration of the broader social determinants of mental health. Research has shown that factors such as income inequality, social isolation, and discrimination play a significant role in mental health outcomes (Marmot, 2005). By focusing solely on individual strategies, the self-help industry risks minimising the impact of these external factors and placing the burden of mental health entirely on the individual.

The focus on individualism in self-help also affects how we understand and address social issues. When personal success is framed as solely the result of individual effort, it becomes easier to blame individuals for their circumstances and ignore the structural inequalities contributing to social problems. This perspective is reflected in the rhetoric of "blaming the victim", a concept introduced by William Ryan in his 1971 book of the same name. Ryan argues that by attributing social problems to the failings of individuals, we absolve society of responsibility for addressing the systemic issues that contribute to those problems. The self-help industry's focus on individualism can reinforce this tendency, leading to a lack of empathy and understanding for those struggling with issues beyond their control.

Moreover, the self-help industry's emphasis on personal responsibility can create unrealistic expectations and place undue pressure on individuals. When people are told that they can achieve anything they set their minds to, they may feel a sense of failure and inadequacy if they fail, even when external factors are at play. This can lead to feelings of shame, guilt, and self-blame, which can exacerbate mental health issues and contribute to a cycle of negative thinking (Ehrenreich, 2009). The self-help industry's failure to acknowledge the role of external factors in shaping our lives can thus have significant emotional and psychological consequences for individuals. To illustrate the limitations of the self-help approach, let's imagine Clara, a mother working two jobs to support her children. Clara turns to self-help books for guidance on improving her financial situation and achieving a better work-life balance. She diligently follows the advice she reads, setting goals, visualising success, and adopting a positive attitude. However, despite her best efforts, she finds herself unable to escape the cycle of poverty. The self-help books she relies on offer little acknowledgement of the structural barriers she faces, such as low wages, lack of affordable childcare, and the absence of social safety nets. As a result, Clara begins to internalise her struggles, believing that her inability to improve her situation reflects her shortcomings. This example highlights how the self-help industry's focus on individualism can obscure the systemic factors that contribute to social problems and place an unfair burden on individuals to overcome challenges beyond their control.

The self-help industry's disregard for external factors is also evident in its treatment of workplace issues. Many self-help books offer advice on succeeding in the corporate world, emphasising the importance of hard work, ambition, and networking. However, these books often ignore the broader organisational and cultural factors impacting career success, such as workplace discrimination, power dynamics, and economic instability. For example, a self-help book might advise women to "lean in" and assert themselves in the workplace without acknowledging the structural barriers women, particularly women of colour, face in advancing their careers (Sandberg, 2014). By focusing solely on individual strategies, the self-help industry can perpetuate the myth that career success is exclusively the result of personal effort, ignoring the systemic inequalities that exist in the workplace.

The self-help industry's failure to address external factors also affects how we approach public policy and social change. When personal success is framed as solely the result of individual effort, there is less incentive to advocate for policies that address the structural issues that contribute to social problems. This perspective can lead to a lack of support for social safety nets, healthcare, education, and other essential public services for addressing inequality and promoting well-being. By promoting an individualistic approach to personal development, the self-help industry can reinforce neoliberal ideologies that prioritise market-based solutions over collective action and social welfare (Giroux, 2015). Furthermore, the self-help industry's focus on individualism can contribute to a culture of self-blame and victim blaming, where individuals are held responsible for their misfortunes, regardless of the external factors at play. This perspective is evident in the rhetoric surrounding issues such as unemployment, homelessness, and addiction, where individuals are often blamed for their circumstances rather than the systemic issues that contribute to these problems. For example, a self-help book might suggest that an unemployed person needs to "think positively" and "work harder" to find a job without acknowledging the impact of economic downturns, automation, and other external factors on the job market. This individualistic approach can lead to a lack of empathy and understanding for those struggling, reinforcing social stigma and making it more challenging to address the root causes of social problems.

The self-help industry's focus on individualism raises ethical concerns, particularly in marketing and promoting self-help products. Many self-help books and programmes are marketed as quick fixes or miracle cures, promising rapid results with minimal effort. This marketing strategy can create unrealistic expectations and encourage people to invest time, money, and emotional energy into products that may not deliver on their promises. When individuals fail to achieve the desired outcomes, they may feel disillusioned and betrayed, leading to further emotional and psychological distress (Illouz, 2008). The self-help industry's emphasis on personal responsibility can also make it difficult for individuals to seek help from others, whether through therapy, social support, or community-based interventions. By promoting an individualistic approach to personal development, the self-help industry can discourage people from reaching out for the support they need, leading to further isolation and disconnection.

# Chapter 6

# Environment Matters

In the bustling self-help marketplace, where motivational books and seminars promise transformative success, a standard narrative persists that individual effort and mindset are the keys to achieving one's goals. While empowering on the surface, this narrative conveniently sidesteps a crucial factor in the success equation: the environment and the context. The self-help industry's focus on individualism can be traced back to neoliberalism's broader cultural and economic context, which emphasises personal responsibility, free-market capitalism, and minimal government intervention (Harvey, 2005). Neoliberalism's ideological underpinnings have profoundly influenced the self-help genre, promoting the idea that individuals are the architects of their destinies. This perspective is appealing because it offers control in an unpredictable world. However, it also perpetuates the myth that success is solely a matter of personal effort, ignoring the systemic and structural factors that shape opportunities and outcomes. While undeniably influential, these texts operate on the premise that success is accessible to anyone who adopts the right mindset and habits. They suggest that wealth, happiness, and personal fulfilment are within reach for those who follow a prescribed set of principles. Yet, these books rarely, if ever, address the environmental constraints that can impede an individual's ability to succeed. Factors such as socioeconomic status, access to quality education, systemic racism, and economic inequality are often absent from the discussion, leaving readers with the impression that failure results from personal shortcomings rather than external barriers (Lipsky, 2010).

Consider the example of socioeconomic status. Research has consistently shown that individuals from lower-income backgrounds face significant obstacles to success, including limited access to resources, fewer educational opportunities, and greater exposure to stressors such as crime and housing instability (Marmot, 2005). These environmental factors can profoundly impact an individual's ability to achieve their goals, yet they are often overlooked in self-help literature. By focusing exclusively on personal responsibility, self-help books can create unrealistic expectations and contribute to feelings of inadequacy among those who cannot overcome the systemic barriers they face. The self-help industry's disregard for environmental factors is particularly evident in its health and well-being treatment. Many self-help books advocate for personal responsibility in managing health, encouraging readers to adopt healthier lifestyles, practise mindfulness, and maintain a positive outlook. While these strategies can be beneficial, they often ignore the social determinants of health – such as income, education, neighbourhood environment, and access to healthcare – that significantly affect health outcomes (Wilkinson & Pickett, 2010). For example, a book promoting healthy eating and regular exercise as the keys to weight loss may be unhelpful, or even harmful, to individuals living in food deserts, where fresh produce is scarce, or those working multiple jobs with little time for exercise. By failing to acknowledge these environmental constraints, self-help books can place an undue burden on individuals to achieve health outcomes that may be beyond their control.

The focus on individualism in self-help literature can also obscure the impact of cultural and social environments on success. Culture shapes our values, beliefs, and behaviours, influencing how we define and pursue success. In collectivist cultures, for example, success may be determined not by individual achievement but by the community's or family's well-being (Triandis, 1995). Yet, many self-help books are rooted in Western individualistic values, promoting autonomy, self-reliance, and personal achievement as the ultimate goals. This cultural bias can make self-help advice irrelevant or counterproductive for individuals from different cultural backgrounds, as it may encourage behaviours that conflict with their cultural norms and values. Moreover, the self-help industry's emphasis on personal responsibility can perpetuate the myth of meritocracy – the belief that anyone can succeed if they work hard. This myth ignores the reality that structural inequalities, such as racism, sexism, and economic disparity, create significant barriers to success for many individuals (McNamee & Miller, 2009). For example, a self-help book that encourages women to "lean in" and assert themselves in the workplace may overlook the systemic discrimination and gender bias that continue to hinder women's advancement in many industries (Sandberg, 2013). By focusing on individual strategies without addressing the broader systemic issues, self-help books can reinforce the status quo and contribute to the marginalisation of already disadvantaged groups.

The self-help industry's failure to consider environmental factors is not just a theoretical concern; it has real-world consequences for individuals who internalise its messages. When people are told they are solely responsible for their success or failure, they may blame themselves for outcomes that are primarily influenced by external factors. This internalisation of failure can lead to shame, guilt, and low self-esteem, particularly among those who face significant environmental barriers to success (Ehrenreich, 2009). For example, an individual who struggles to find employment in a depressed job market may be led to believe that their inability to secure a job is due to a lack of effort or motivation rather than the economic conditions that limit job opportunities. This self-blame can have detrimental effects on mental health and well-being, contributing to a cycle of negative thinking and learned helplessness.

In addition to the psychological impact, the self-help industry's focus on individualism can have broader social and political implications. By framing success as a matter of personal responsibility, self-help books can obscure the need for collective action and systemic change. If individuals believe their success is entirely within their control, they may be less likely to support policies addressing the structural inequalities that contribute to social problems. This perspective aligns with neoliberal ideology, which emphasises individualism and free-market solutions while downplaying the role of government and collective action in addressing social issues (Giroux, 2008). The result is a society where individuals are encouraged to "fix" themselves rather than work together to create a more just and equitable world.

The self-help industry's neglect of environmental factors also raises ethical concerns. Many self-help books are marketed as quick fixes or miracle cures, promising rapid results with minimal effort. This marketing strategy can create unrealistic expectations and encourage people to invest time, money, and emotional energy into products that may not deliver on their promises. When individuals fail to achieve the desired outcomes, they may feel disillusioned and betrayed, leading to further emotional and psychological distress (Illouz, 2008). The industry's emphasis on personal responsibility can also discourage individuals from seeking help from others, whether through therapy, social support, or community-based interventions. By promoting an individualistic approach to personal development, the self-help industry can contribute to a culture of self-blame and victim blaming, where individuals are held responsible for their misfortunes, regardless of the external factors at play.

The threads of social, cultural, and economic contexts are not mere background noise; they are the fabric that shapes our experiences, identities, and opportunities. Yet, in a world increasingly obsessed with individualism, self-improvement, and personal responsibility, these crucial elements are often relegated to the sidelines or dismissed as secondary or irrelevant. In popular culture and self-help literature, the notion of the "self-made individual" looms large. This archetype, celebrated in countless books, films, and motivational speeches, portrays success as the result of sheer willpower, determination, and personal grit. The narrative is simple and seductive: anyone can achieve greatness if they work hard enough, think positively, and take control of their destiny. For instance, Bronfenbrenner's (1979) ecological systems theory posits that individuals are nested within multiple layers of environmental influence, ranging from immediate settings like family and school to broader societal and cultural contexts. These environments interact with one another and the individual, creating a dynamic system that shapes development and behaviour. Ignoring these contexts, as the self-made individual narrative often does, is akin to studying a fish without considering the water in which it swims.

Social context refers to the web of relationships and social structures surrounding us. It encompasses everything from family dynamics and peer groups to institutional systems and societal norms. Social context profoundly influences our opportunities, choices, and outcomes. Consider the role of social capital, a concept popularised by sociologist Pierre Bourdieu (1986). Social capital refers to the resources we can access through our social networks – information, support, and opportunities. Individuals with substantial social capital are more likely to succeed in various domains, from education to employment, because they can leverage their connections to gain advantages. Conversely, those with weak social capital may struggle to access the same opportunities, regardless of their efforts or abilities. Research has shown that social capital can significantly impact life outcomes. For example, Putnam (2000) found that communities with high levels of social capital tend to have lower crime rates, better health outcomes, and higher levels of civic engagement. This suggests that success is not just a matter of individual effort but is also contingent on the social environment in which one is embedded.

Cultural context refers to the shared values, beliefs, and practices that characterise a group or society. Culture shapes how we see the world, how we interact with others, and what we consider essential. It influences our goals, behaviour, and understanding of success and failure. One of the most significant ways culture influences behaviours is through the concept of cultural capital, another of Bourdieu's (1986) key contributions. Cultural capital refers to the knowledge, skills, and behaviours that are valued in a particular society and used to gain social mobility. For example, in many Western cultures, individuals familiar with higher education norms – who know how to speak the language of academia, navigate the bureaucracy of universities, and engage in scholarly discourse – are more likely to succeed in academic settings. Those who lack this cultural capital, often because they come from backgrounds where higher education is less familiar or valued, may struggle to succeed, even if they possess the same intellectual abilities as their peers. Cultural context also shapes our understanding of identity and self. Markus and Kitayama (1991) introduced the concept of independent and interdependent self-construal to explain how cultural differences influence self-perception. In individualistic cultures, like many Western countries, people are likelier to see themselves as independent agents responsible for their success and failure. In collectivist cultures, common in many Asian and African societies, individuals are more likely to see themselves as interconnected with others, with success and failure being shared among family or community members.

These cultural differences have profound implications for how we approach life's challenges. In individualistic cultures, the emphasis on personal responsibility can lead to more significant stress and anxiety when individuals fail to meet their goals, as they may feel that they have only themselves to blame. In collectivist cultures, the emphasis on community and interdependence can provide a buffer against stress, as individuals feel supported by their social networks. However, it can also create pressure to conform to group norms, potentially stifling individual creativity and ambition. Economic context refers to the material conditions of life – income, wealth, employment, and access to resources. It is the most visible and measurable of the contexts discussed here, and its impact on success is profound and well documented. The most apparent way economic context influences success is through access to resources. Individuals from wealthier backgrounds typically have access to better education, healthcare, and housing. They are more likely to live in safe neighbourhoods, attend well-funded schools, and receive support that fosters academic and professional success (Marmot, 2005). Conversely, individuals from poorer backgrounds often face significant barriers to success, including underfunded schools, limited access to healthcare, and neighbourhoods plagued by crime and violence.

Economic inequality also affects psychological well-being. Wilkinson and Pickett (2009) found that societies with high levels of economic inequality tend to have higher rates of mental illness, drug abuse, and crime. This suggests that economic context not only influences material outcomes but also shapes the psychological and emotional landscape in which people live. Individuals from lower-income backgrounds may experience social exclusion and stigmatisation, leading to a reduction in social capital and cultural capital. They may also internalise negative cultural stereotypes about poverty, leading to feelings of shame and low self-worth (Lott, 2002). These factors can create a vicious cycle where economic disadvantage leads to social and cultural exclusion, perpetuating economic disadvantage.

The self-help industry, with its relentless focus on individualism, often ignores these interactions between social, cultural, and economic contexts. By promoting the idea that success is solely a matter of personal effort, self-help books and programmes can create unrealistic expectations and contribute to a culture of blame. When individuals fail to achieve their goals, they may internalise the belief that they are solely responsible for their failure, leading to feelings of inadequacy and despair. The focus on individualism can obscure the need for systemic change. If success is seen as solely a matter of personal responsibility, there is little motivation to address the structural inequalities that create barriers to success for so many people. This can perpetuate the status quo, allowing unchallenged social, cultural, and economic disparities to persist. In a society that values fairness and equality, individual effort should not determine success. While personal responsibility is essential, it must be understood within the broader social, cultural, and economic forces that shape our lives. Only by acknowledging and addressing these forces can we create a society where everyone has the opportunity to succeed.

As we move forward, developing a more nuanced understanding of success is essential – one that recognises the importance of social, cultural, and economic contexts. This requires a shift from the simplistic, individualistic narratives the self-help industry promotes towards a more comprehensive approach that considers environmental factors. In education, for example, we must recognise that students' success is not just a matter of personal effort but is also shaped by the available resources and opportunities. This means addressing inequalities in school funding, providing support for students from disadvantaged backgrounds, and creating educational environments that are inclusive and culturally responsive. In the workplace, we must acknowledge that employees' performance is influenced by their social and cultural capital and economic circumstances. This means creating more equitable hiring practices, providing training and support for employees from diverse backgrounds, and fostering inclusive workplace cultures. In health care, we must recognise that the social determinants of health shape individuals' health outcomes. This means addressing the root causes of health disparities, such as poverty, racism, and lack of access to care, rather than placing the burden of health solely on individual behaviour.

## How Self-Help Ignores or Minimises Structural Inequalities

With its pervasive influence and seductive promises of personal transformation, the self-help industry operates on a fundamental premise: individuals possess the power to shape their destinies through sheer willpower, positive thinking, and a disciplined approach to life. While appealing in its simplicity, this premise overlooks a critical dimension of human experience – structural inequalities. These systemic barriers shape and constrain individual opportunities, often along race, class, gender, and other social identities. As a professor of community psychology, I contend that by ignoring or minimising these structural inequalities, the self-help industry not only perpetuates a myth of personal agency but also reinforces the systems of oppression it purports to help individuals overcome.

At the heart of the self-help industry is individualism – the belief that personal success or failure is determined primarily by individual effort and choices. This perspective aligns closely with neoliberal ideologies, emphasising personal responsibility, free markets, and minimal government intervention. Neoliberalism posits that individuals are rational actors who can succeed by making the right choices, working hard, and staying motivated (Harvey, 2005). The self-help industry echoes these sentiments, offering many books, seminars, and online courses designed to help individuals optimise their lives and achieve success, regardless of their starting point.

However, this focus on individualism is deeply problematic because it ignores the reality of structural inequalities. Structural inequalities refer to the systematic disadvantages that certain groups face due to their social identities, such as race, gender, or socioeconomic status. These inequalities are not the result of individual failings but are embedded in the social, economic, and political systems that govern society. For example, people of colour in many societies face significant barriers to education, employment, and housing due to systemic racism. Similarly, women often encounter gender discrimination that limits their opportunities for career advancement and economic security (Crenshaw, 1991).

By promoting the idea that success is solely a matter of personal effort, the self-help industry fails to acknowledge the significant role that these structural factors play in shaping individuals' lives. This oversight can lead to the harmful implication that those who fail are simply not trying hard enough, thereby blaming the victim rather than addressing the root causes of inequality. Self-help literature often erases or downplays the importance of social context in shaping individual outcomes. This erasure is evident in the genre's focus on techniques like positive thinking, visualisation, and goal setting, which are seen as universally applicable strategies for success. While these techniques may be helpful for some individuals, they fail to account for the different starting points and systemic barriers that people face.

For instance, a self-help book encouraging readers to "think positively" and "visualise success" may resonate with someone with access to education, stable employment, and a supportive social network. However, for someone living in poverty, facing discrimination, or dealing with chronic illness, these strategies may feel irrelevant or even insulting. The suggestion that they can overcome their challenges simply by changing their mindset ignores the complex social and economic factors contributing to their situation (Lilienfeld, 2007).

The emphasis on personal responsibility in self-help literature can reinforce the idea that individuals are solely to blame for their circumstances. This narrative is particularly detrimental because it shifts attention away from the systemic issues that create and maintain inequality. For example, when self-help books promote the idea that anyone can achieve financial success by adopting the proper habits, they obscure the fact that economic mobility is often limited by factors such as access to quality education, social capital, and discrimination in the labour market (Marmot, 2005). This erasure of social context distorts the reality of inequality. It perpetuates the myth of meritocracy – the false belief that everyone has an equal opportunity to succeed if they work hard enough.

The self-help industry thrives on the commodification of hope – the idea that individuals can purchase the tools, knowledge, or mindset needed to overcome challenges and achieve success. This commodification is evident in the vast array of self-help products, from books and online courses to coaching sessions and motivational seminars. These products often come with a hefty price tag, which raises important questions about who benefits from the self-help industry and who is left behind. One fundamental critique of the self-help industry is that it often targets middle- and upper-class consumers with the financial means to invest in self-improvement. These consumers are more likely to have the resources, time, and social capital needed to benefit from self-help strategies. In contrast, individuals from lower-income backgrounds may struggle to afford these products, and even if they can, they may find that the advice offered does not resonate with their lived experiences or address the structural barriers they face (McGee, 2005). The commodification of hope can lead to a cycle of dependency, where individuals continue to purchase self-help products to find the "magic bullet" that will solve their problems. This cycle is fuelled by the self-help industry's tendency to offer quick fixes and simple solutions, which can create unrealistic expectations and lead to disappointment and disillusionment when these solutions fail to deliver the promised results (Illouz, 2008). In this way, the self-help industry not only capitalises on individuals' desire for self-improvement but also reinforces the inequalities it claims to address by placing the burden of change on individuals rather than on the systems perpetuating inequality.

For example, self-help books that focus on building confidence or improving communication skills may be helpful for individuals who are already privileged in terms of their social identity and economic status. However, for marginalised individuals, these books may fail to address the specific barriers they face, such as racial or gender discrimination, language barriers, or lack of access to resources. In these cases, the advice offered by self-help books may be ineffective and harmful, as it can lead to feelings of frustration, inadequacy, and self-blame when individuals cannot achieve the desired outcomes (Hooks, 2000). The oversimplification of self-help literature can lead to a lack of critical engagement with the root causes of inequality. By focusing on individual behaviour and mindset, self-help books often neglect the broader social, economic, and political factors contributing to inequality. This lack of critical engagement can perpetuate the status quo by promoting the idea that individuals can overcome systemic barriers through personal effort alone, thereby absolving society of the responsibility to address these barriers through collective action and systemic change.

In its focus on individualism and personal responsibility, the self-help industry can inadvertently perpetuate inequality by reinforcing the systems of oppression it seeks to challenge. This perpetuation of inequality occurs in several ways. First, by promoting the idea that success is solely a matter of individual effort, the self-help industry reinforces the myth of meritocracy – the belief that everyone has an equal opportunity to succeed if they work hard enough. This myth obscures the reality of structural inequalities and allows those who are privileged to attribute their success to their efforts rather than to the advantages they have received (Littler, 2017). In this way, the self-help industry can perpetuate inequality by legitimising the status quo and discouraging critical engagement with the social and economic systems that maintain inequality. Second, the self-help industry's focus on individualism can lead to a lack of solidarity and collective action. When individuals are encouraged to focus solely on their success and personal development, they may be less likely to engage in collective efforts to address systemic issues. This focus on individualism can undermine social movements and community organising efforts to challenge inequality and promote social justice (Putnam, 2000). By promoting a narrow, individualistic approach to success, the self-help industry can contribute to the fragmentation of social movements and the weakening of collective efforts to create a more just and equitable society. The self-help industry's commodification of hope can exacerbate economic inequality by placing the burden of change on individuals rather than on the systems perpetuating inequality. When individuals are encouraged to purchase self-help products to achieve success, they may be less likely to advocate for systemic changes that would benefit everyone. This focus on individual solutions can divert attention and resources away from efforts to address the root causes of inequality, thereby perpetuating the inequalities the self-help industry claims to address.

## What About Social Change?

In an era where individualism is frequently lauded as the ultimate pathway to success, the essential role of community and systemic change in achieving genuine social progress is often overlooked. The self-help industry, focusing on personal responsibility and individual achievement, epitomises this trend by offering solutions that place the onus entirely on the individual while ignoring the broader social, cultural, and economic contexts in which people live. However, as a critical community psychologist, I argue that meaningful and sustainable change cannot occur in isolation. Instead, it necessitates a collective approach that acknowledges the interconnectedness of individuals and the systemic structures that shape their lives.

The ethos of individualism, which permeates much of Western culture, is predicated on the belief that each person is the architect of their destiny. This worldview posits that success is achieved through hard work, determination, and self-discipline, while failure is attributed to a lack of effort or personal shortcomings. While this narrative can be empowering, it is also profoundly flawed because it disregards the systemic barriers that limit opportunities for many individuals. As sociologist Robert D. Putnam (2000) argues, the decline of social capital and community engagement has eroded the collective support systems that once enabled individuals to thrive. Putnam's work highlights how the disintegration of communal ties has led to increased social isolation and the weakening of the bonds that once held communities together. The self-help industry, with its focus on personal empowerment, reinforces this individualistic mindset by offering solutions that are narrowly focused on the individual. Books, seminars, and online courses often emphasise the importance of setting personal goals, developing a positive mindset, and cultivating self-discipline as the keys to success. While these strategies can be beneficial, they fail to address the systemic factors contributing to social inequality and limiting individual agency. For instance, a person may be encouraged to "think positively" and "work harder". Still, these efforts are unlikely to yield significant results if they are constrained by systemic issues such as poverty, discrimination, or lack of access to education and healthcare (Marmot, 2005).

Structural inequalities refer to the systemic disparities in access to resources, opportunities, and power that are often based on social categories such as race, class, gender, and disability. These inequalities are not merely the result of individual failings but are embedded in the very fabric of society, shaping the opportunities available to different groups of people. As a community psychologist, it is crucial to recognise that these structural factors profoundly influence individual behaviour and outcomes. For example, research has shown that socioeconomic status is a significant determinant of health outcomes, with lower-income individuals experiencing higher rates of chronic illness, shorter life expectancy, and greater exposure to environmental hazards (Wilkinson & Pickett, 2009). The self-help industry's failure to address these structural inequalities perpetuates the myth that individuals are solely responsible for their success or failure; this narrative places an unfair burden on individuals and obscures the need for systemic change. As Bell Hooks (2000) argues, true liberation cannot be achieved through individual efforts alone; it requires a collective movement that challenges and dismantles the oppressive systems perpetuating inequality. Hooks's work underscores the importance of viewing individual struggles within the broader context of societal structures and emphasises the necessity of community and collective action in achieving social justice. While individual efforts can undoubtedly contribute to personal growth and development, they do not address the root causes of social problems. Collective action, on the other hand, has the potential to create meaningful and lasting change by challenging the systemic structures that maintain inequality. History is replete with examples of social movements that have successfully brought about systemic change through collective action. The Civil Rights Movement, the Women's Suffrage Movement, and the Labor Movement are examples of how organised, collective efforts have led to significant social, political, and economic reforms.

Collective action is not just about mobilising large groups to protest or demand change; it is also about building and sustaining communities that can support individuals in their efforts to achieve personal and social well-being. Community-based interventions, for example, effectively address a wide range of social issues, from reducing crime rates to improving public health outcomes. These interventions are often successful because they recognise that individuals do not exist in isolation but are part of more extensive social networks that influence their behaviour and well-being (Wandersman & Florin, 2003). Empowerment is not just about giving people the tools to succeed independently but also about creating conditions that allow individuals and communities to thrive. This requires addressing the structural barriers that limit opportunities and working to create more equitable and just systems. As Julian Rappaport (1987) notes in his seminal work on empowerment theory, "Empowerment is not something that can be given to people; it is something that people must claim for themselves." Rappaport's work highlights the importance of collective action and community organising in empowering individuals and communities to achieve social change.

One of the significant shortcomings of the self-help industry is its tendency to offer universal solutions to problems that are deeply rooted in specific social, cultural, and economic contexts. While the advice to "be positive" or "set goals" may resonate with some individuals, it may be irrelevant or even harmful to others facing different challenges or operating within different cultural frameworks. For instance, a self-help book that emphasises the importance of assertiveness may be counterproductive in cultures that value collectivism and social harmony over individual assertiveness (Markus & Kitayama, 1991). To be truly effective, interventions to promote individual and community well-being must be tailored to the specific contexts in which people live. This means considering the social, cultural, and economic factors influencing behaviour and opportunities. For example, public health interventions that are designed to reduce smoking rates must consider the social and economic factors that contribute to smoking, such as poverty, stress, and targeted advertising by the tobacco industry. Simply telling individuals to "quit smoking" without addressing these underlying factors is unlikely to be effective (Marmot & Wilkinson, 2006).

Moreover, the self-help industry's focus on individualism can exacerbate feelings of isolation and disconnection, particularly in communities with weak social support networks. Research has shown that social support is a critical determinant of mental and physical health, with individuals with strong social ties experiencing better health outcomes and greater resilience in the face of adversity (Cohen, 2004). By encouraging individuals to focus solely on their success and well-being, the self-help industry may inadvertently undermine the social connections that are essential for individual and community health. While individual efforts are significant, they are not enough to address interconnected social problems such as the lack of affordable housing and the mental distress that poor housing can cause for people. Systemic change is necessary to create conditions where all individuals and communities can thrive. This requires a shift away from the narrow focus on individualism and personal responsibility that characterises much of the self-help industry and towards a more holistic approach that recognises the importance of social, cultural, and economic context. Systemic change involves addressing the structural inequalities that limit opportunities and challenging the cultural narratives that perpetuate these inequalities. For example, the narrative of meritocracy – the belief that everyone has an equal opportunity to succeed if they work hard – must be challenged to create a more just and equitable society. Research has shown that meritocracy is a myth that obscures the reality of structural inequalities and reinforces the status quo (Littler, 2017). By challenging this narrative and promoting a more nuanced understanding of success and failure, we can create the conditions for systemic change.

In addition to challenging cultural narratives, systemic change also requires implementing policies and practices that promote equity and social justice. This may involve redistributing resources, reforming institutions, and creating new, more inclusive, and participatory systems of governance. For example, policies that promote affordable housing, access to education, and fair wages are essential for addressing the root causes of inequality and creating a more just and equitable society (Wilkinson & Pickett, 2009). One of the most critical aspects of community and systemic change is the creation of communities of resistance and resilience. These communities resist the forces of oppression and inequality and build the capacity to thrive in the face of adversity. Building such communities requires a commitment to solidarity, mutual aid, and collective action. Communities of resistance and resilience are not just about surviving in the face of oppression; they are also about creating new ways of living and being rooted in the principles of equity, justice, and sustainability. This involves challenging the dominant cultural narratives that prioritise individualism, consumerism, and competition and instead promoting cooperation, solidarity, and collective well-being. One example of a community of resistance and resilience is the Black Lives Matter movement, which has mobilised millions of people around the world to challenge systemic racism and police violence. The movement has raised awareness of these issues and created spaces for collective action, mutual aid, and community building. By centring the voices and experiences of marginalised communities, Black Lives Matter has challenged the dominant narratives perpetuating racism and inequality and created a powerful force for systemic change (Garza, 2020).

# Chapter 7

# Mental Health, Therapy, and the Limits of Self-Help

The unregulated nature of life coaching allows anyone to assume the title of "life coach" without formal qualifications, training, or certification. This lack of oversight results in considerable variability in the competence of life coaches, which can lead to inconsistent and, at times, harmful practices. Life coaching remains unregulated. Unlike other helping professions such as psychology, counselling, or social work, life coaching does not require practitioners to obtain a formal licence or certification or adhere to a specific code of ethics (that was the case at the time of the publication of this book). This absence of regulation means that anyone, regardless of their educational background or experience, can call themselves a life coach and offer services to the public (Grant, 2017). The lack of standardised requirements for entry into the profession is deeply concerning because it opens the door for individuals without adequate knowledge or training to provide advice and guidance that could significantly impact clients' lives. Clients may be unaware of the differences between a licensed mental health professional and an unlicensed life coach, leading to confusion about the qualifications and expertise of the person they entrust with their personal development. This confusion can be worsened because life coaches often employ language and techniques like those of trained psychologists or counsellors, blurring the line between coaching and therapy (Spence & Grant, 2007). Without regulation, there is no formal mechanism to distinguish between life coaches with relevant qualifications and those without, leaving their clients vulnerable to potentially ineffective or damaging interventions.

The lack of standardisation in life coaching extends beyond regulation to the variability in training and competence among practitioners. While some life coaches may have robust backgrounds in psychology, counselling, or related fields, others may have little to no relevant training. The inconsistency in life coaches' educational and experiential backgrounds leads to significant disparities in the quality of service provided. Research by Grant and Cavanagh (2011) highlights that most life coaches have received training through short-term certification programmes that vary widely in depth and rigour. These programmes, which are often unaccredited and lacking in comprehensive curriculum standards, may provide a superficial understanding of coaching techniques with little emphasis on the ethics.

The variability in training raises severe concerns about the ability of life coaches to support their clients effectively and safely. Unlike psychologists or counsellors, who undergo extensive training and supervision in diagnosing and treating mental health issues, many life coaches are not equipped to recognise or address psychological distress. This knowledge gap can lead to situations where life coaches inadvertently harm their clients by offering inappropriate advice or failing to refer them to qualified mental health professionals when necessary. For example, a life coach without adequate training might misinterpret a client's symptoms of depression or anxiety as a lack of motivation or willpower, leading to interventions that exacerbate the client's condition. The absence of standardised training means that life coaches may lack a solid foundation in evidence-based practices. In psychology and counselling, practitioners are trained to rely on research-supported interventions and critically evaluate their methods' effectiveness. However, in life coaching, there is no guarantee that coaches are using approaches that have been empirically validated. Instead, many life coaches rely on anecdotal evidence or popular self-help theories that may not have been subjected to rigorous scientific scrutiny (Grant, 2003). This reliance on untested methods can result in interventions that are not only ineffective but potentially harmful, particularly for vulnerable groups who may benefit from mental health care specialists.

The potential for harm in an unregulated life coaching industry is significant, particularly given the power dynamics inherent in the coach-client relationship. Life coaches often position themselves as experts in personal development, wielding considerable influence over their clients' decisions and behaviours. However, without a regulatory framework to ensure that coaches are acting in their clients' best interests, there is a risk that some coaches may exploit this power for financial gain or personal satisfaction rather than prioritising the well-being of their clients (Berglas, 2002). The lack of oversight also means that clients have limited recourse if they feel mistreated or the coaching they received was ineffective or harmful. One of the most concerning aspects of the unregulated life coaching industry is the potential for coaches to unintentionally cause harm by overstepping their professional boundaries. For example, a life coach without sufficient psychological training may attempt to address issues such as trauma, addiction, or mental illness, areas that require specialised knowledge and skills. In such cases, the coach's interventions may not only fail to help the client but could also exacerbate their condition, leading to further psychological distress (Spence, Cavanagh, & Grant, 2008). Additionally, the absence of a regulatory body means there is no standard procedure for addressing ethical violations, leaving clients vulnerable to unethical practices such as breaches of confidentiality, inappropriate relationships, or financial exploitation. Given the significant risks associated with life coaching's unregulated nature, there is a compelling need for regulation and standardisation within the industry. Establishing minimum educational and training requirements for life coaches would help ensure that practitioners have a foundational understanding of psychological principles, ethical guidelines, and evidence-based practices. Moreover, implementing a licensure system like those in place for psychologists and counsellors would provide a formal mechanism for holding life coaches accountable for their professional conduct and the quality of their services.

## What About Pop Psychology?

In today's fast-paced, social media-saturated world, the attraction of pop psychology is hard to resist. While pop psychology can serve as an entry point to more profound psychological knowledge, it carries significant dangers, particularly regarding the potential for misinformation, the promotion of superficial solutions, and the tendency to reinforce harmful stereotypes and societal norms. Pop psychology refers to psychological concepts, theories, and advice that are simplified, often oversimplified, and presented in a way that is accessible to the public, typically through mass media, self-help books, and social media platforms. These ideas are frequently distilled into easy-to-understand tips and strategies. While pop psychology can make psychological knowledge more accessible, it often lacks the depth and rigour of academic psychology and may spread misinformation or reinforce stereotypes.

Pop psychology distils complex psychological concepts into catchy phrases and relatable anecdotes, making it seem as though the mysteries of the human mind can be unravelled with just a few simple tips or strategies. Pop psychology often appeals to our desire for quick fixes. In a world where time is scarce, many people are drawn to the promise of immediate results. Whether it's a book that claims to teach you how to be happier in seven days or a TED Talk that guarantees to boost your productivity with just one simple habit, pop psychology offers attainable and time-efficient solutions. This appeal is further amplified by the ubiquitous nature of social media, where psychological advice is often condensed into bite-sized nuggets that can be consumed in seconds.

However, it is precisely this accessibility and emphasis on quick fixes that contribute to the dangers of pop psychology. By reducing psychological phenomena to simplistic explanations and solutions, pop psychology risks spreading misinformation, promoting ineffective or harmful interventions, and reinforcing harmful societal norms. One of the most significant dangers of pop psychology is its potential to spread misinformation. In the pursuit of making psychological concepts more accessible, pop psychology often oversimplifies or distorts these concepts to the point where they no longer accurately reflect the current state of psychological science. This is particularly problematic when pop psychology presents itself as authoritative and scientific, leading the public to believe that the information they are receiving is grounded in empirical research when, in fact, it may not be. A prime example of this is the widespread popularity of the "left-brain versus right-brain" theory, which claims that individuals are either left-brained (logical, analytical) or right-brained (creative, intuitive). While this theory has been debunked by neuroscientists who have shown that both brain hemispheres engage in nearly all cognitive tasks (Nielsen et al., 2013), it remains a staple of pop psychology. The persistence of this myth illustrates how easily misinformation can take hold in the public consciousness, particularly when it is presented in a way that resonates with people's desire for simple explanations of their behaviour.

Another example of misinformation in pop psychology is the pervasive myth of "learning styles". The idea that individuals learn best when information is presented in their preferred learning style (e.g., visual, auditory, kinesthetic) has been widely promoted in educational and psychological contexts. However, research has consistently shown little evidence to support the effectiveness of tailoring instruction to learning styles and that such practices may even be counterproductive (Pashler et al., 2008). Despite this, the learning styles myth continues to be propagated in pop psychology, demonstrating how easily unsubstantiated claims can gain traction when not critically examined. By offering quick fixes often devoid of context or nuance, pop psychology can create the illusion that deep-seated issues can be resolved with minimal effort. This is particularly concerning when it comes to mental health, where pop psychology often suggests that conditions such as depression or anxiety can be overcome simply by "thinking positively" or "changing your mindset".

While it is accepted that cognitive-behavioural techniques, such as reframing negative thoughts, can be helpful for some individuals, pop psychology's emphasis on positive thinking as a cure-all can be harmful. For one, it can lead individuals to blame themselves if they are unable to "think their way" out of a mental health condition, thereby exacerbating feelings of guilt and inadequacy. Moreover, by promoting the idea that positive thinking alone is sufficient to overcome mental health challenges, pop psychology may discourage individuals from seeking out more comprehensive treatment, such as therapy or medication, which could be more effective in addressing their needs (Ehrenreich, 2009). The promotion of superficial solutions is not limited to mental health. Pop psychology offers overly simplistic advice on various issues, from relationships to career success. For example, many pop psychology books and articles advise individuals to "follow their passion" for career fulfilment. While this advice may resonate with some, it ignores the realities of the job market and economic constraints. Not everyone has a transparent or financially viable passion to pursue. By offering such simplistic advice, pop psychology risks setting people up for disappointment and failure when the promised outcomes do not materialise. In addition to spreading misinformation and promoting superficial solutions, pop psychology also risks reinforcing harmful stereotypes and societal norms. This is particularly evident in how it often frames success, happiness, and well-being in individualistic terms, downplaying the role of social, cultural, and structural factors in shaping people's lives.

Much of pop psychology is predicated on personal responsibility – that individuals have complete control over their happiness and success and that failure to achieve these goals reflects personal shortcomings. While it is essential to recognise individuals' agency in their lives, this narrative can be harmful when it ignores the broader social and structural factors that influence outcomes. For instance, telling someone in poverty they need to adopt a "success mindset" to improve their circumstances overlooks the systemic barriers that may hold them back, such as lack of access to education, healthcare, and economic opportunities (Prilleltensky, 2012). Pop psychology often reinforces gender stereotypes by promoting traditional roles and expectations. For example, many self-help books aimed at women emphasise the importance of nurturing, empathy, and support, while books aimed at men often promote assertiveness, competitiveness, and emotional stoicism. These gendered messages can reinforce harmful stereotypes and limit individuals' ability to express their full range of emotions and behaviours, perpetuating inequality (Gilligan, 1982). Pop psychology also upholds societal norms regarding body image, appearance, and consumerism. The proliferation of self-help books and programmes focused on weight loss, beauty, and material success often promotes the idea that personal worth is tied to external achievements and physical appearance. This can contribute to the internalisation of unrealistic and harmful standards, leading to issues such as body dissatisfaction, low self-esteem, and disordered eating (Stice & Shaw, 2002).

One underlying factor driving pop psychology's dangers is its commercialisation. In a consumer-driven society, there is a significant profit motive behind producing and disseminating pop psychology content. Publishers, authors, and media outlets are incentivised to create content that will sell, even if that content is oversimplified or inaccurate. This profit motive can lead to the commodification of psychological knowledge, where concepts are packaged and sold as easily consumable products. The commercialisation of psychology is evident in the proliferation of self-help books, seminars, and online courses that promise to provide the "secret" to happiness, success, or personal fulfilment. These products often come with hefty price tags, further reinforcing the idea that psychological well-being can be bought rather than cultivated through meaningful engagement with oneself and one's community. Moreover, the focus on individual success and self-improvement in pop psychology aligns with the values of neoliberalism, which emphasises personal responsibility, competition, and consumerism. The danger of this commercialisation is that it can lead to the exploitation of vulnerable individuals seeking solutions to their problems. People who are struggling with mental health issues, relationship difficulties, or career challenges may turn to pop psychology for guidance, only to be met with advice that is not only ineffective but also potentially harmful. In this way, pop psychology can exacerbate the issues it claims to address, leading to a cycle of dependence on superficial solutions that do not address the root causes of people's problems.

## Examples of Effective Community-Based Interventions

Community-based interventions offer a promising alternative by addressing the root causes of these issues within the context of the communities affected. Before delving into specific examples, it is essential to understand why community-based interventions are so crucial. Unlike individual-focused approaches, which often place the burden of change solely on the individual, community-based interventions recognise that individuals are deeply embedded in social, cultural, and economic contexts. These interventions aim to address the systemic factors contributing to social problems by involving the community in designing, implementing, and sustaining solutions. One of the fundamental principles of community psychology is the emphasis on empowerment, which involves enabling individuals and communities to take control of their lives and influence the systems that affect them. Empowerment cannot be handed down from above; the community itself must claim it through collective action and participation. As Rappaport (1987) notes, "Empowerment is both a value orientation for working in the community and a theoretical model for understanding the process by which people gain control over their lives" (p. 122). Community-based interventions, therefore, offer a more holistic and sustainable approach to addressing social problems by fostering empowerment and promoting social justice.

## Example 1: The Harlem Children's Zone

One of the most well-known examples of an effective community-based intervention is the Harlem Children's Zone (HCZ) in New York City. Founded by Geoffrey Canada in 1997, HCZ is a comprehensive, community-wide effort to break the cycle of poverty and improve educational outcomes for children in Harlem. The initiative combines various services, including early childhood education, parenting workshops, after-school programmes, and health services, to create a supportive environment for children and families. The success of HCZ lies in its holistic approach, which recognises that children's educational outcomes cannot be improved in isolation from the broader social and economic conditions in which they live. By addressing multiple aspects of a child's life – such as health, family stability, and neighbourhood safety

– HCZ creates a "pipeline" of support that follows children from birth through college. This comprehensive approach has significantly improved educational outcomes, with HCZ students outperforming their peers in standardised tests and achieving higher graduation rates (Dobbie & Fryer, 2011). It is important to critically examine HCZ's limitations. While the initiative has successfully improved educational outcomes for many children in Harlem, it is also resource-intensive, relying on substantial private and public funding. This raises questions about the scalability and sustainability of such interventions, particularly in underfunded communities. Additionally, some critics argue that while HCZ has succeeded in creating opportunities for individual children, it has not addressed the broader structural inequalities that perpetuate poverty in Harlem (Tough, 2008).

## Example 2: The Brazilian Community Health Agent Program

The Brazilian Community Health Agent Program (CHAP) is another example of an effective community-based intervention that addresses health disparities in low-income communities. Established in 1991, CHAP recruits and trains community members to serve as health agents who provide essential health services, health education, and referrals to medical professionals in their neighbourhoods. The programme aims to improve access to healthcare in underserved areas and promote preventive health practices within the community. One of CHAP's key strengths is its emphasis on community participation and the use of local knowledge. By recruiting community members as health agents, the programme ensures that the services provided are culturally appropriate and responsive to the community's specific needs. Research has shown that CHAP has successfully reduced infant mortality rates, improved vaccination coverage, and increased access to prenatal care in low-income communities in Brazil (Macinko et al., 2007). CHAP also faces challenges, particularly regarding sustainability and scalability. The programme relies heavily on government funding and support, making it vulnerable to political and economic changes. Additionally, while CHAP has successfully improved access to healthcare, it has not fully addressed the broader social determinants of health, such as poverty and education, that contribute to health disparities (Victora et al., 2011). This highlights the need for a more integrated approach that combines health interventions with efforts to address the underlying social and economic conditions that affect health outcomes.

### Example 3: Participatory Budgeting in Porto Alegre

Participatory budgeting (PB) is a democratic process that allows community members to participate directly in the allocation of public funds. One of the most successful examples of PB is the initiative in Porto Alegre, Brazil, which began in 1989. In this process, residents of Porto Alegre are allowed to participate in public meetings where they discuss and decide on allocating a portion of the city's budget. The initiative aims to increase transparency, accountability, and community involvement in local governance. The success of PB in Porto Alegre lies in its ability to empower community members and increase their influence over public policy. Research has shown that PB has led to a more equitable distribution of resources, with funds directed towards underserved communities and infrastructure improvements, such as sanitation and transportation, which benefit the broader population (Baiocchi, 2003). Additionally, PB has strengthened the relationship between the government and the community, fostering a sense of ownership and accountability among residents. However, PB also faces limitations, particularly regarding participation and representation. While PB has successfully engaged a broad cross-section of the community, there are still challenges in ensuring that marginalised groups, such as women, ethnic minorities, and low-income residents, have an equal voice in the decision-making process (Wampler, 2007). Additionally, PB requires a significant investment of time and resources from the government and the community, raising questions about its sustainability and scalability in other contexts.

## Example 4: The Kibera Slum Upgrading Project

The Kibera Slum Upgrading Project (KSUP) in Nairobi, Kenya, is another example of an effective community-based intervention that addresses the challenges faced by residents of informal settlements. Launched in 2004, KSUP aims to improve living conditions in Kibera – one of Africa's largest slums – by providing access to essential services, such as water, sanitation, and housing, and promoting economic development through microfinance and entrepreneurship programmes. One of KSUP's key strengths is its emphasis on community participation and collaboration with local organisations. The project involves residents in the planning and implementation of upgrades, ensuring that the solutions are tailored to the community's specific needs and priorities. This participatory approach has led to significant improvements in living conditions, with residents gaining access to clean water, sanitation facilities, and improved housing (Huchzermeyer, 2011). However, KSUP also faces challenges, particularly regarding land tenure and displacement. While the project has improved living conditions for many residents, it has also displaced some families who could not afford the upgraded housing. This raises questions about the intervention's social equity and the need for more comprehensive solutions that address the root causes of informal settlement growth, such as poverty and lack of affordable housing (Huchzermeyer, 2011).

## Lessons Learned

The examples of community-based interventions discussed in this chapter offer valuable lessons for future initiatives. One key takeaway is the importance of community participation and empowerment in ensuring the success and sustainability of interventions. By involving community members in designing, implementing, and evaluating interventions, these initiatives are more likely to be culturally appropriate, responsive to local needs, and sustainable over the long term. Another important lesson is the need for a holistic and integrated approach to addressing social problems. While each of the interventions discussed has successfully addressed specific issues, they have also faced challenges in addressing the broader systemic factors that contribute to these problems. This highlights the importance of combining community-based interventions with efforts to address the underlying social, economic, and political conditions that perpetuate inequality. Finally, the examples discussed in this chapter underscore the need for flexibility and adaptability in community-based interventions. Each community is unique, with its own set of challenges, resources, and priorities. Effective interventions must be tailored to the specific context in which they are implemented and flexible enough to adapt to changing conditions and needs.

## Conclusion: Community, Connection, and Collective Action

In a world increasingly dominated by individualism, the notion of community has sometimes been relegated to the margins of public discourse. Yet, as we navigate the complexities of contemporary life – marked by social inequality, mental health crises, environmental degradation, and political polarisation – it becomes evident that the solutions to our most pressing problems lie not in the isolated efforts of individuals but in the collective power of communities. As a community psychologist, I argue that we must rekindle our understanding of the importance of community, connection, and collective action to address these real-world challenges effectively. Self-help perpetuates specific cultural narratives, particularly the idea of the "self-made" individual. This narrative emphasises personal responsibility and success due to individual effort. An example of how self-help perpetuates the cultural narrative of the "self-made" individual can be seen in the book *The 7 Habits of Highly Effective People* by Stephen R. Covey. This self-help book promotes the idea that personal and professional success results from individual habits, choices, and discipline. Covey's framework emphasises personal responsibility, suggesting that anyone can succeed by adopting certain habits and principles regardless of external circumstances. This narrative reinforces the cultural belief that success is primarily a product of individual effort and self-determination, downplaying the role of systemic factors such as socioeconomic background, access to education, or social support networks. This focus on personal agency aligns with the broader cultural ideal of the "self-made" person, who rises to success through hard work and determination. It often promotes a highly individualistic approach to solving personal problems, which can contradict more collectivist or community-oriented values. This emphasis on individualism reinforces neoliberal ideologies prioritising personal achievement over collective well-being. The focus on self-improvement can weaken social bonds and community ties, as individuals are encouraged to prioritise personal success over communal support. This shift impacts social cohesion and community resilience. The materials are often more accessible to those with financial resources, perpetuating social stratification. Self-help promotes a highly individualistic approach that may contradict more collectivist values in the book *You Are a Badass* by Jen Sincero. This book encourages readers to take control of their lives through self-belief, self-empowerment, and personal responsibility, often framing success as a matter of mindset and individual effort. The book's emphasis on personal achievement and wealth-building aligns with neoliberal ideologies prioritising individual success over collective well-being. This focus on self-improvement subtly suggests that personal issues are best solved by looking inward and focusing on one's goals rather than seeking communal support or considering broader social responsibilities. This approach can weaken social bonds by encouraging people to prioritise their success over the group's well-being in communities where collectivist values, such as mutual aid and communal support, are vital. The self-help industry, which often targets middle-class or affluent audiences, tends to be more accessible to those with financial resources, thereby perpetuating social stratification by providing these tools to those who can afford them.

This dynamic can further deepen inequalities, as those with fewer resources may lack access to the same level of self-improvement materials, reinforcing existing social divides. Self-help caters to mostly middle-class individuals and diverts attention away from systemic reform, as shown in the book *The Secret* by Rhonda Byrne. This book popularised the concept of the "law of attraction", suggesting that individuals can attract wealth, health, and happiness by simply thinking positively and visualising success. The message is highly individualistic, focusing on personal mindset and attitudes as the key to solving life's problems while ignoring the structural barriers and systemic inequalities many face, such as poverty, lack of access to education, or discriminatory practices. *The Secret* primarily appeals to middle-class readers with some degree of financial stability, as it assumes that individuals have the time, energy, and resources to focus on self-visualisation and personal development. This narrative can be exclusionary for those from lower socio-economic backgrounds who may be struggling with basic survival needs and do not have the luxury of engaging in such practices. By promoting the idea that success and well-being are solely the result of personal effort and mindset, the book absolves institutions like governments and corporations from responsibility for addressing broader social issues. It shifts the focus away from the need for systemic reforms, such as improving access to education, healthcare, and fair wages, reinforcing the status quo and diverting attention away from the structural changes necessary to create a more equitable society. The self-help industry often overlaps with workplace productivity culture, promoting concepts like "hustle" and "grind" that align with capitalist demands for efficiency and profit. Self-help can frequently reinforce traditional gender roles. These materials might emphasise traits like passivity, emotional labour, and appearance, perpetuating societal expectations. This can shape modern identities, encouraging people to see themselves as projects to be continually improved. It imposes Western notions of success, happiness, and individuality on diverse cultures. While self-help offers accessible tools for personal growth, often grounded in cognitive-behavioural techniques, the effectiveness of self-help frequently hinges on an individual's motivation and ability to apply strategies consistently. However, without professional guidance, there's a risk of misinterpretation or unmet expectations. The commercialisation of the self-help industry raises ethical concerns about the quality and credibility of the advice given.

Before exploring the importance of community and collective solutions, it is essential to critique the pervasive myth of individualism. Research in community psychology has consistently demonstrated that individual behaviour cannot be fully understood without considering the broader social, economic, and cultural contexts in which it occurs (Prilleltensky, 2003). For instance, an individual's health is not solely determined by personal choices but is also influenced by factors such as access to healthcare, economic stability, education, and social support. Ignoring these factors leads to an incomplete and often misguided understanding of human behaviour and well-being. The fallacy of individualism also manifests in the self-help industry, which frequently promotes the idea that personal transformation is a matter of willpower and mindset alone. While self-help can provide valuable tools for personal growth, it often fails to acknowledge individuals' structural barriers, such as poverty, discrimination, and lack of access to resources (Illouz, 2008). By placing the onus of change entirely on the individual, this industry perpetuates the myth that personal failures result from inadequate effort rather than systemic inequities.

## The Power of Community and Connection

In contrast to the isolating effects of individualism, communities provide a vital source of connection, support, and resilience. Humans are inherently social creatures, and our well-being is deeply intertwined with our relationships and social networks (Cohen, 2004). Communities offer a sense of belonging, identity, and purpose, which is essential for psychological and emotional well-being. This is particularly important in times of crisis, when individuals may feel overwhelmed by their challenges. The importance of community is evident in research on social support, which consistently shows that strong social ties are associated with better mental and physical health outcomes (Berkman, Glass, Brissette, & Seeman, 2000). For example, studies have found that individuals with strong social support networks are less likely to experience depression, anxiety, and stress and are more likely to recover from illness and adversity (Uchino, 2009). These findings underscore the importance of fostering and maintaining community connections as a protective factor against life's challenges. Communities are not just sources of support but also powerful agents of change.

Throughout history, collective action has been a driving force behind social movements that have challenged injustice, inequality, and oppression. From the civil rights movement in the United States to the struggle against apartheid in South Africa, communities have mobilised to demand and achieve systemic change (Tarrow, 2011). These movements were not the result of isolated individuals working independently but of communities coming together to confront shared challenges and advocate for collective solutions.

Real-world problems often require solutions that are beyond the capacity of any individual. Climate change, for instance, is a global issue that demands coordinated action at multiple levels – local, national, and international. While individual actions, such as reducing one's carbon footprint, are essential, they are insufficient to address the problem's scale. Instead, collective action, such as policy advocacy, community organising, and international cooperation, is necessary to drive the systemic changes needed to mitigate the impacts of climate change (Klein, 2014). Similarly, poverty, inequality, and social injustice cannot be resolved through individual efforts alone. These problems are deeply embedded in social and economic structures that perpetuate wealth, power, and opportunity disparities. As such, they require collective solutions that address the root causes of these inequalities. For example, participatory budgeting, a process in which community members have a direct say in allocating public funds, has been shown to reduce poverty and improve public services in cities worldwide (Wampler, 2007). This approach empowers communities to take control of their resources and make decisions that reflect their needs and priorities. In Brazil, implementing the Family Health Program, which provides primary healthcare services at the community level, has significantly improved health outcomes, particularly in low-income areas (Macinko, Almeida, & de Sá, 2007). By involving community members in planning and delivering healthcare services, this programme has improved access to care and built trust and engagement within the community.

The Harlem Children's Zone, a community-based organisation in New York City, provides comprehensive support to children and families in one of the city's most underserved neighbourhoods. Through education, healthcare, and social services, the Harlem Children's Zone has significantly improved educational outcomes and reduced poverty in the community (Tough, 2008). This success is a testament to the power of collective action and the importance of addressing the social determinants of well-being. Another example is Slum Dwellers International (SDI), a network of community-based organisations that advocate for the rights of people living in informal settlements worldwide. Through collective action, SDI has successfully secured land rights, improved living conditions, and influenced housing policy in numerous countries (Cities with 'slums', 2023). These achievements highlight the importance of community organising and collective solutions in addressing the challenges faced by marginalised populations. As we look to the future, the challenges we face will require even greater emphasis on community and collective action. The COVID-19 pandemic has laid bare the deep inequalities and vulnerabilities in our societies, highlighting the need for coordinated responses that prioritise the well-being of all community members. At the same time, the pandemic also demonstrated the power of collective action, as communities worldwide came together to support one another, advocate for equitable policies, and demand accountability from their governments. The climate crisis, too, will require unprecedented levels of cooperation and collective action. While individual actions are necessary, they must be part of a broader strategy that includes local, national, and global systemic changes. This will require not only political will but also the active engagement of communities in advocating for and implementing sustainable solutions.

## Mattering and Belonging:
## The Cornerstones of Human Well-Being

In a world that often prioritises achievement over connection and competition over collaboration, mattering and belonging have become of renewed importance in the discourse on human well-being. These are not just abstract ideas confined to philosophical debate; they are the bedrock of our psychological health, social cohesion, and survival as a species. As a community psychologist, I must delve deeply into these concepts, challenging the prevailing narratives that often minimise their significance. Mattering and belonging are not just nice-to-have aspects of life – they are fundamental human needs, intricately tied to our identity, motivation, and overall sense of purpose. Mattering is a concept that, on the surface, seems straightforward: it is the feeling that we are significant in the lives of others and that our existence impacts the world around us. But mattering goes beyond mere significance; it is about being seen, valued, and recognised for who we are, not just what we do. This concept was first articulated by Rosenberg and McCullough (1981), who identified mattering as a central human need, on a par with Maslow's (1943) hierarchy of needs. However, unlike Maslow's model, which has been critiqued for its individualistic and Western-centric biases (Koltko-Rivera, 2006), the concept of mattering inherently acknowledges the social nature of human beings: "...the perception that, to some degree and in any of a variety of ways, we are a significant part of the world around us" (Elliot, Kao, & Grant, 2004, p. 339).

Mattering can be broken down into three key components: attention, importance, and reliance (Elliott, 2009). Attention refers to the feeling that others notice and care about our well-being. Importance is the belief that others value us and that our contributions are meaningful. Reliance involves the sense that others depend on us, which fosters a feeling of responsibility and purpose. Together, these components create a sense of mattering that is vital for psychological well-being. The absence of mattering can lead to feelings of invisibility and insignificance, which are often precursors to mental health issues such as depression and anxiety (Taylor & Turner, 2001). In extreme cases, the lack of mattering can contribute to social isolation, which has been shown to have severe implications for both mental and physical health (Cacioppo & Cacioppo, 2014). Therefore, fostering environments where individuals feel they matter is not just a moral imperative but a public health necessity. "Mattering is the feeling of being significant and important to other people" (Flett & Nepon, p. 667).

Closely related to mattering is the concept of belonging. While mattering is about feeling significant, belonging is about feeling connected. It is the sense that we are part of a group, community, or society that accepts us for who we are. Belonging is a fundamental human need, as articulated by Baumeister and Leary (1995), who argued that belonging is a powerful, pervasive, and primary human motivation. According to their research, belongingness is not just about social interaction but about forming meaningful, lasting relationships that provide a sense of security and identity. The importance of belonging is evident in various social and psychological outcomes. People who feel a strong sense of belonging are more likely to experience positive mental health, including lower levels of depression and anxiety, higher self-esteem, and greater life satisfaction (Hagerty et al., 1996). On the other hand, those who experience social exclusion or lack a sense of belonging are at a higher risk for mental health problems and even physical health issues, such as increased inflammation and weakened immune function (Eisenberger & Cole, 2012). Belonging is not just about fitting in; it is about being accepted and valued within a community that shares our values and goals. This is why belonging is often tied to identity – our sense of who we are is intricately linked to the groups we belong to (Tajfel & Turner, 1986). When we belong to a group that values us, we experience a sense of security and self-worth. Conversely, our sense of identity and self-esteem can be severely compromised when we are excluded or marginalised.

Mattering and belonging are deeply interconnected. While mattering gives us the sense that we are essential and have a role to play, belonging provides the social context in which that role can be enacted. In other words, mattering gives us purpose and belonging provides us with a place to fulfil that purpose. Together, they create a synergistic relationship that is essential for individual and collective well-being. This synergy is particularly evident in community settings. When individuals feel they matter to their community and belong within it, they are more likely to contribute to the collective good. This can lead to higher levels of civic engagement, social cohesion, and collective efficacy – the belief that the community can work together to achieve common goals (Sampson, Raudenbush, & Earls, 1997). Conversely, when people feel that they do not matter or do not belong, they are more likely to disengage from the community, leading to social fragmentation and the erosion of social capital (Putnam, 2000).

The importance of mattering and belonging is not limited to local communities; it also extends to larger social and political contexts. For example, research has shown that political engagement is higher among individuals who feel they matter to the political process and belong to a political community (Dalton, 2008). This suggests that fostering a sense of mattering and belonging can have far-reaching implications for the health of our democracies. As a discipline, community psychology is uniquely positioned to address the importance of mattering and belonging. Unlike traditional psychology, which often focuses on individual behaviour in isolation, community psychology emphasises the social and environmental factors contributing to well-being (Rappaport, 1987). This holistic approach recognises that personal well-being is deeply intertwined with the community's well-being. Empowerment is connected to mattering and belonging because it fosters a sense of agency and purpose within a supportive social context. When people feel empowered, they are more likely to believe that they matter and belong, enhancing their motivation to contribute to the community. Community psychology also emphasises the importance of social justice, which involves addressing the structural inequalities that undermine mattering and belonging. For example, marginalised groups often face systemic barriers that prevent them from feeling that they matter or that they belong. These barriers include discrimination, poverty, and lack of resource access (Prilleltensky, 2008). By advocating for policies and practices that promote inclusion and equity, community psychologists can help create environments where everyone can feel that they matter and belong.

The importance of mattering and belonging will only continue to grow. In an increasingly interconnected and globalised world, our challenges – such as climate change, social inequality, and political polarisation – will require collective solutions rooted in a shared purpose and identity. Fostering mattering and belonging will be essential for building the social cohesion and collective efficacy to address these challenges. At the same time, the rise of digital technologies and social media presents opportunities and challenges for fostering mattering and belonging. On the one hand, these technologies can connect people across geographic and cultural boundaries, creating new opportunities for belonging. On the other hand, they can also contribute to social fragmentation and the erosion of meaningful connections (Turkle, 2011). We can be mindful of these dynamics and work to ensure that digital spaces are inclusive and supportive environments where everyone can feel that they matter and belong.

In a world increasingly dominated by individualism, where personal success and self-sufficiency are often glorified, community, mattering, and belonging can sometimes seem like quaint notions from a bygone era. However, as this chapter has argued, these concepts are not merely nostalgic ideals but fundamental components of human well-being. The solutions to these challenges might not lie in the isolated efforts of individuals but in the collective power of communities, where people feel they matter, belong, and have the power to effect change. The pervasive myth of individualism, which suggests that all success and failure are the results of personal effort alone, has been critiqued extensively in community psychology. Research consistently shows that individual behaviour cannot be fully understood without considering the broader social, economic, and cultural contexts in which it occurs. This critique extends to the self-help industry, which often promotes the idea that personal transformation is simply a matter of willpower and mindset. While there is some value in personal development, this approach frequently overlooks the structural barriers – such as poverty, discrimination, and lack of access to resources – that limit opportunities for many individuals. By placing the burden of change solely on the individual, the self-help industry perpetuates a misguided understanding of human potential and well-being, reinforcing the myth that personal failures are due to insufficient effort rather than systemic inequities.

Humans are social creatures, and our well-being is deeply intertwined with our relationships and social networks. Communities provide a sense of belonging, identity, and purpose and a crucial buffer against life's challenges. Research on social support has consistently demonstrated that strong social ties are associated with better mental and physical health outcomes. In times of crisis, whether personal or collective, our connections with others help us navigate adversity and emerge stronger on the other side. However, communities are not just passive sources of support but also active agents of change. Throughout history, collective action has been the driving force behind social movements that have challenged injustice, inequality, and oppression. From the civil rights movement in the United States to the struggle against apartheid in South Africa, communities have come together to demand and achieve systemic change. These movements were successful not because of isolated individual efforts but because of the collective power of people who believed they mattered, felt they belonged to a more significant cause, and were empowered to act.

Issues like climate change, poverty, and social injustice are deeply embedded in social and economic structures and require collective solutions. For example, while individual actions to reduce carbon footprints are necessary, they are insufficient to address the global scale of climate change. Coordinated action at the local, national, and international levels is essential to drive the systemic changes needed to mitigate the impacts of climate change (Klein, 2014). Similarly, addressing poverty and inequality requires solutions that go beyond personal responsibility. Participatory budgeting, for instance, empowers communities to take control of public funds and make decisions that reflect their needs and priorities, leading to tangible improvements in public services and reducing poverty (Wampler, 2007).

The examples of the Harlem Children's Zone and Slum Dwellers International (SDI) illustrate the transformative power of community-based initiatives. The Harlem Children's Zone provides comprehensive support to children and families in one of New York City's most underserved neighbourhoods, significantly improving educational outcomes and reducing poverty (Tough, 2008). SDI, a network of community-based organisations advocating for the rights of people living in informal settlements, has successfully secured land rights, improved living conditions, and influenced housing policy in numerous countries (Cities with 'slums', 2023). These achievements underscore the importance of collective action and community organising in addressing the challenges faced by marginalised populations.

The challenges we face – whether related to public health, social justice, or environmental sustainability – will require even greater emphasis on community and collective action. The COVID-19 pandemic, for example, exposed deep inequalities and vulnerabilities in our societies, highlighting the need for coordinated responses that prioritise the well-being of all community members. At the same time, the pandemic also showed the power of collective action, as communities worldwide came together to support one another, advocate for equitable policies, and hold governments accountable. The climate crisis is another area where collective action will be essential. While individual efforts to live more sustainably are significant, they must be part of a broader strategy that includes local, national, and global systemic changes. This will require not only political will but also the active engagement of communities in advocating for and implementing sustainable solutions. The stakes are high, but the potential for positive change is enormous if we can harness the power of community and collective action.

When people feel they matter and belong, they are more likely to contribute to the common good, leading to more robust, more cohesive communities. Conversely, when people feel excluded or marginalised, the entire community suffers from social fragmentation and the erosion of trust and cooperation. We are critical in fostering environments where people feel they matter and belong. This involves supporting individuals and advocating for policies and practices that promote inclusion, equity, and social justice. It means recognising that individual well-being is deeply intertwined with the community's well-being and that citizens' participation can be necessary to address our existential challenges. The importance of community, connection, and collective action cannot be overstated. As we navigate the uncertainties and challenges of the twenty-first century, these concepts will be essential for building resilient, inclusive, and just societies. The solutions to our most pressing problems lie not in the isolated efforts of individuals but in the collective power of communities where people feel they matter, belong, and have the power to effect change.

## Conclusion

The self-help industry is worth billions, has garnered considerable popularity over recent decades. Its personal empowerment, happiness, and success promises have become a staple of modern culture. However, the industry perpetuates neoliberal individualism, ignores structural inequalities, and commodifies mental health, offering only superficial solutions to deeply rooted societal problems. At the heart of the self-help industry lies an ideology of individualism, which aligns seamlessly with neoliberal values. Neoliberalism, a political and economic philosophy prioritising free markets, competition, and minimal government intervention, puts the burden on individuals' success over their well-being squarely. This ethos is deeply ingrained in self-help literature, which often espouses the idea that anyone can succeed if they only work hard enough, think positively, or adopt the right habits. Books from the genre encapsulate this belief, claiming that personal prosperity results from individual effort, mindset, and willpower. However, the focus on individual responsibility obscures the structural and systemic barriers many people face. Poverty, racism, sexism, and other forms of discrimination create obstacles that no amount of positive thinking or personal ambition can surmount. The self-help industry's emphasis on personal responsibility often leads to victim blaming, wherein individuals are made to feel that their struggles are solely the result of their failings rather than the product of larger societal forces. This perspective is not only psychologically harmful but also counterproductive in addressing the root causes of mental health issues and inequality.

People do not exist in a vacuum; they are influenced by their environments, social networks, and the institutions that shape their lives. From this standpoint, the self-help industry's narrow focus on individual change is inadequate. It fails to address the structural determinants of mental health, such as unemployment, housing instability, and social exclusion, which can have far more profound effects on well-being than any self-help technique. For instance, self-help books often advocate for resilience, mindfulness, or time-management skills to reduce stress or burnout. While these strategies may be helpful in some cases, they ignore the fact that many people experience anxiety because of systemic issues like precarious employment, low wages, or lack of access to healthcare. Focusing solely on individual coping strategies distracts from the need for collective action and structural change. Instead of encouraging people to adapt to unjust systems, the goal should be to challenge and transform those systems to promote mental health and well-being for all. The industry thrives on selling solutions to personal problems, often framing them in simplistic and consumer-friendly terms. This commodification turns mental health into a product to be bought and sold, with success stories usually predicated on purchasing the right book, attending a suitable seminar, or subscribing to the right programme. This commercialisation of mental health is problematic for several reasons. First, it reduces complex psychological and social issues to readily marketable products, offering quick fixes that often fail to address the underlying causes of distress. Second, it privileges those who can afford to participate in the self-help economy, creating a form of "well-being privilege" where access to mental health resources is contingent upon one's financial means. This exclusionary aspect of the industry contradicts the principles of community psychology, which advocates for equitable access to mental health care and resources.

Additionally, the commodification of self-help often leads to a "blame the victim" mentality. When individuals invest in self-help products and do not achieve the promised results, they may internalise feelings of failure, believing they did not try hard enough or lacked the necessary personal qualities. This can exacerbate feelings of isolation and self-doubt, further entrenching the very issues the self-help industry claims to solve. A critical community psychologist would argue that mental health should not be treated as a commodity but as a fundamental human right, requiring collective investment in social services, healthcare, and community support systems. One of the self-help industry's main selling points is the promise of empowerment. It claims to give individuals the tools and knowledge they need to take control of their lives, achieve their goals, and overcome obstacles. However, this empowerment is often misguided. Empowerment involves increasing individuals' capacity to effect change in their lives, communities, and society. It facilitates collective agency, challenges power structures, and promotes social justice. In contrast, the self-help industry's version of empowerment is individualistic and depoliticised. It encourages people to focus on personal success and self-improvement, often at the expense of collective well-being. Moreover, the solutions offered by self-help literature are frequently superficial, addressing symptoms rather than causes. Empowerment cannot be achieved through individualistic pursuits alone; it requires collective action and social change. The self-help industry's emphasis on individual transformation distracts from the need to address the structural inequalities that limit true empowerment for many people. The importance of social connections and support networks in promoting mental health and well-being must be at the forefront together with recognising that individuals thrive in supportive, inclusive, and empowered communities where they can access resources and participate in collective decision-making processes. The self-help industry often promotes an atomised vision of self-improvement, where individuals are solely responsible for their success or failure. Such a focus on individualism neglects the importance of community and social support in supporting well-being. It reinforces the myth of the "self-made" person, ignoring the role relationships, social networks, and community resources play in personal development and success. Can well-being be achieved in isolation? It requires healthy and supportive communities and collective action to address the structural determinants of health and well-being.

# References

Alexander, M. (2010). *The New Jim Crow: Mass Incarceration in the Age of Colorblindness*. The New Press.

Amabile, T., & Kramer, S. (2011). *The Progress Principle: Using Small Wins to Ignite Joy, Engagement, and Creativity at Work*. Harvard Business Press.

American Psychological Association. (2018). Stress in America: Generation Z. Accessed from https://www.apa.org/news/press/releases/stress/2018/stress-gen-z.pdf

Anderson, P. (2022) NPD BookScan: US 2021 Market Unit Volume Up 9 Percent [Accessed 01/08/2024] https://publishingperspectives.com/2022/01/npd-bookscan-american-market-unit-volume-up-9-percent-in-2021-covid19/#:~:text=Print%20book%20sales%20by%20volume,as%20the%20leading%20growth%20category.

Autor, D. H. (2014). "Polanyi's Paradox and the Shape of Employment Growth". NBER Working Paper No. 20485. *National Bureau of Economic Research*. https://doi.org/10.3386/w20485

Autor, D. H., Dorn, D., & Hanson, G. H. (2013). "The China Syndrome: Local Labor Market Effects of Import Competition in the United States". *American Economic Review*, 103(6), 2121–2168. https://doi.org/10.1257/aer.103.6.2121

Baiocchi, G. (2003). Participation, Activism, and Politics: The Porto Alegre Experiment. Deepening Democracy: Institutional Innovations in Empowered Participatory Governance, 45–76. https://doi.org/10.4324/9780203496411

Barry, A., Osborne, T., & Rose, N. (2013). *Foucault and Political Reason: Liberalism, Neo-Liberalism and the Rationalities of Government*. Routledge.

Baumeister, R. F., & Leary, M. R. (1995). "The Need to Belong: Desire for Interpersonal Attachments as a Fundamental

Human Motivation". *Psychological Bulletin*, 117(3), 497–529. https://doi.org/10.1037/0033-2909.117.3.497

Berglas, S. (2002). "The Very Real Dangers of Executive Coaching". *Harvard Business Review*, 80(6), 86–92.

Berkman, L. F., Glass, T., Brissette, I., & Seeman, T. E. (2000). "From Social Integration to Health: Durkheim in the New Millennium". *Social Science & Medicine*, 51(6), 843–857. https://doi.org/10.1016/S0277-9536(00)00065-4

Bertrand, R. (1972). In Praise of Idleness and Other Essays. Unwin paperbacks

Bourdieu, P. (2011). "The Forms of Capital". (1986). In *Cultural Theory: An Anthology*, 1(81–93), 949.

Bronfenbrenner, U. (1979). *The Ecology of Human Development: Experiments by Nature and Design.* Harvard University Press google schola, 2, 139–163.

Brown, B. (2018). *Dare to Lead: Brave Work. Tough Conversations. Whole Hearts.* Random House.

Brown, W. (2015). *Undoing the Demos: Neoliberalism's Stealth Revolution.* Mit Press.

Bureau of Labor Statistics. (2021). Union Members – 2021. U.S. Department of Labor. Retrieved from https://www.bls.gov/news.release/pdf/union2.pdf

Byrne, R. (2006). *The Secret.* Atria Books.

Cacioppo, J. T., & Cacioppo, S. (2014). "Social Relationships and Health: The Toxic Effects of Perceived Social Isolation". *Social and Personality Psychology Compass*, 8(2), 58–72. https://doi.org/10.1111/spc3.12087

Cederström, C. (2015). *The Wellness Syndrome* (Vol. 94). Polity Press.

Chancel, L., Piketty, T., Saez, E., Zucman, G., Alvaredo, F., Atkinson, A. B., & Morelli, S. (2022). World Inequality Report 2022. World Inequality Lab. Retrieved from https://wir2022.wid.world/

Chou, H. T. G., & Edge, N. (2012). "'They are happier and having better lives than I am': The impact of using Facebook on perceptions of others' lives". *Cyberpsychology, Behavior, and Social Networking*, 15(2), 117–121.

Cohen, J. (2004). "Parasocial breakup from favorite television characters: The role of attachment styles and relationship intensity". *Journal of Social and Personal Relationships*, 21(2), 187–202.

Cohen, S. (2004). "Social relationships and health". *American Psychologist*, 59(8), 676–684. https://doi.org/10.1037/0003-066X.59.8.676

Coyne, J. C., & Tennen, H. (2010). "Positive psychology in cancer care: Bad science, exaggerated claims, and unproven medicine". *Annals of Behavioral Medicine*, 39(1), 16–26

Cruikshank, B. (1999). *The Will to Empower: Democratic Citizens and Other Subjects*. Cornell University Press.

Cuijpers, P., & Schuurmans, J. (2007). "Self-help interventions for anxiety disorders: an overview". *Current Psychiatry Reports*, 9, 284–290.

Cuijpers, P., Karyotaki, E., Weitz, E., Andersson, G., Hollon, S. D., & van Straten, A. (2014). "The effects of psychotherapies for major depression in adults on remission, recovery and improvement: a meta-analysis". *Journal of Affective Disorders*, 159, 118–126.

Dalton, R. J. (2008). *The Good Citizen: How a Younger Generation Is Reshaping American Politics*. CQ Press.

Diener, E., & Seligman, M. E. P. (2004). "Beyond Money: Toward an Economy of Well-Being". *Psychological Science in the Public Interest*, 5(1), 1–31.

Dobbie, W., & Fryer, R. G. (2011). "Are high-quality schools enough to close the achievement gap? Evidence from a social experiment in Harlem". *American Economic Journal: Applied Economics*, 3(3), 158–187. https://doi.org/10.1257/app.3.3.158

Dutton, J. E., & Ragins, B. R. (Eds.). (2017). *Exploring Positive Relationships at Work: Building a Theoretical and Research Foundation*. Psychology Press.

Economic Policy Institute. (2015). The Productivity–Pay Gap. Retrieved from https://www.epi.org/productivity-pay-gap/

Ehrenreich, B. (2009). *Bright-Sided: How the Relentless Promotion of Positive Thinking Has Undermined America*. Metropolitan Books.

Elliott, G. C. (2009). *Family Matters: The Importance of Mattering to Family in Adolescence*. Wiley-Blackwell.

Elliott, G., Kao, S., & Grant, A. M. (2004). "Mattering: Empirical validation of a social-psychological concept". *Self and Identity*, 3(4), 339–354.

Esser, J. K., & Lindoerfer, J. S. (1989). "Groupthink and the space shuttle Challenger accident: Toward a quantitative case analysis". *Journal of Behavioral Decision Making*, 2(3), 167–177.

Fisher, A. (2017). "Toxic positivity at work: The problem with always trying to be positive". *Harvard Business Review*. Retrieved from https://hbr.org/

Flett, G. L., & Nepon, T. (2019). The development and psychometric properties of the Anti-Mattering Scale as a measure of feeling insignificant to other people. [Manuscript in preparation].

Foucault, M. (1977). *Discipline and Punish: The Birth of the Prison*. Pantheon Books.

Fox, D. R., Austin, S., & Prilleltensky, I. (2009). *Critical Psychology: An Introduction*. Sage

Freire, P. (1970). *Pedagogy of the Oppressed*. Continuum.

Friedman, M. (2017). *Hustle: The Myth of Endless Work and the Pathways to Happiness*. University of Chicago Press.

Furedi, F. (2004). *Therapy Culture: Cultivating Vulnerability in an Uncertain Age*. Routledge.

Gans, H. J. (1995). *The War Against the Poor. The Underclass and Antipoverty Policy*. BasicBooks, 10 East 53rd Street, New York, NY 10022-5299.

Garza, A. (2020). *The Purpose of Power: How We ComeTtogether When We Fall Apart*. One World.

Gauntlett, D. (2008). *Media, Gender and Identity: An introduction.* Routledge.

Giroux, H. A. (2008). *Against the Terror of Neoliberalism: Politics Beyond the Age of Greed.* Paradigm Publishers.

Global Market Insights. (2021). E-Learning Market Size by Technology. [Accessed 08/08/2024] from https://www.gminsights.com/industry-analysis/e-learning-market-size

Global Wellness Institute. (2021). The Global Wellness Economy: Looking Beyond COVID. [Accessed 08/08/2024] from https://globalwellnessinstitute.org/industry-research/global-wellness-economy

Goodman, R. T. (2008). Against the Terror of Neoliberalism: Politics Beyond the Age of Greed. Symploke, 16(1/2), 354.

Grant, A. M. (2003). "The impact of life coaching on goal attainment, metacognition and mental health". *Social Behavior and Personality: An International Journal*, 31(3), 253–263.

Grant, A. M. (2017). "The third 'generation' of workplace coaching: creating a culture of quality conversations". *Coaching: An International Journal of Theory, Research and Practice*, 10(1), 37–53.

Guthman, J. (2011). *Weighing In: Obesity, Food Justice, and the Limits of Capitalism* (Vol. 32). University of California Press.

Hafer, C. L., & Sutton, R. (2016). Belief in a just world. Handbook of social justice theory and research, 145–160.

Hagerty, B. M., Williams, R. A., Coyne, J. C., & Early, M. R. (1996). Sense of belonging and indicators of social and psychological functioning. Archives of Psychiatric Nursing, 10(4), 235–244. https://doi.org/10.1016/S0883-9417(96)80029-X

Harvey, D. (2005). *A Brief History of Neoliberalism.* Oxford University Press.

Holt-Lunstad, J., Smith, T. B., & Layton, J. B. (2010). "Social relationships and mortality risk: a meta-analytic review". *PLoS Medicine*, 7(7), e1000316.

hooks, b. (2000). *All About Love: New Visions.* William Morrow.

hooks, b. (2000). *Feminist Theory: From Margin to Center*. Pluto Press.

Huchzermeyer, M. (2011). *Cities with 'slums': From informal settlement eradication to a right to the city in Africa*. University of Cape Town Press.

Illouz, E. (2008). *Saving the Modern Soul: Therapy, Emotions, and the Culture of Self-Help*. University of California Press.

Janis, I. L. (1972). Victims of groupthink: A psychological study of foreign-policy decisions and fiascoes. Houghton Mifflin.

Klein, N. (2014). *This Changes Everything: Capitalism vs. the Climate*. Simon & Schuster.

Koltko-Rivera, M. E. (2006). "Rediscovering the later version of Maslow's hierarchy of needs: Self-transcendence and opportunities for theory, research, and unification". *Review of General Psychology*, 10(4), 302–317. https://doi.org/10.1037/1089-2680.10.4.302

Kozol, J. (1991). *Savage Inequalities: Children in America's chools*. Crown.

Ladson-Billings, G. (2006). "From the achievement gap to the education debt: Understanding achievement in US schools". *Educational Researcher*, 35(7), 3–12.

Lasch C. (1979). *The Culture of Narcissism: American life in an Age of Diminishing Expectations*. New York: Norton.

Lilienfeld, S. O. (2005). "Scientifically unsupported and supported interventions for childhood psychopathology: A summary". *Pediatrics*, 115(3), 761–764.

Lilienfeld, S. O. (2007). "Psychological treatments that cause harm". *Perspectives on Psychological Science*, 2(1), 53–70.

Littler, J. (2017). *Against Meritocracy: Culture, Power and Myths of Mobility*. Taylor & Francis.

Lott, B. (2002). "Cognitive and behavioral distancing from the poor". *American Psychologist*, 57(2), 100.

Macinko, J., Almeida, C., & de Sá, P. K. (2007). A rapid assessment methodology for the evaluation of primary care organization and performance in Brazil. Health Policy and Planning, 22(3), 167–177. https://doi.org/10.1093/heapol/czm009

Macinko, J., Almeida, C., & de Sá, P. K. (2007). "Organization and delivery of primary health care services in Petrópolis, Brazil". International Journal of Health Services, 37(3), 533–551. https://doi.org/10.2190/HS.37.3.g

Marketdata LLC. (2020). The U.S. Market for Self-Improvement Products & Services. [Accessed 08/08/2024] https://wifitalents.com/statistic/personal-development-industry/#:~:text=The%20personal%20development%20market%20in%20North%20America%20is%20expected%20to,at%20%2432.14%20billion%20in%202020.

Markus, H. R., & Kitayama, S. (2014). "Culture and the Self: Implications for Cognition, Emotion, and Motivation". College Student Development and Academic Life. Routledge. (pp. 264–293).

Marmot, M. (2005). "Social determinants of health inequalities". The Lancet, 365(9464), 1099–1104. https://doi.org/10.1016/S0140-6736(05)74234-3

Marmot, M. (2005). The Status Syndrome: How Social Standing Affects Our Health and Longevity. Bloomsbury Press.

Marmot, M., & Wilkinson, R. G. (2006). Social Determinants of Health. Oxford University Press.

Maslach, C., & Leiter, M. P. (2016). "Understanding the burnout experience: Recent research and its implications for psychiatry". World Psychiatry, 15(2), 103–111.

Maslow, A. H. (1943). "A Theory of Human Motivation". Psychological Review, 1, 943.

Masters, R. A. (2010). Spiritual Bypassing: When Spirituality Disconnects Us from What Really Matters. North Atlantic Books.

McGee, M. (2005). Self-Help, Inc.: Makeover Culture in American Life. Oxford University Press.

Mishel, L., Gould, E., & Bivens, J. (2015). "Wage Stagnation in Nine Charts". *Economic Policy Institute*. Retrieved from https://www.epi.org/publication/charting-wage-stagnation/

Nelson, G., & Prilleltensky, I. (Eds.). (2010). *Community Psychology: In Pursuit of Liberation and Well-Being*. Palgrave Macmillan.

Newport, C. (2016). *Deep Work: Rules for Focused Success in a Distracted World*. Hachette UK.

Norcross, J. C., & Hill, C. E. (2002). "Empirically Supported Therapy Relationships". In Psychotherapy Relationships That Work, CE Hill 1–16.

Paul't Hart. (1991). "Irving L. Janis' victims of groupthink". *Political Psychology*, 247–278.

Peale, N. V. (2012). *The Power of Positive Thinking*. Touchstone.

Peck, J. (2001). *Workfare States*. Guilford Press.

Piketty, T. (2014). *Capital in the Twenty-First Century*. Harvard University Press.

Prilleltensky, I. (2003). "Understanding, resisting, and overcoming oppression: Toward psychopolitical validity". *American Journal of Community Psychology*, 31(1–2), 195–201. https://doi.org/10.1023/A:1023043108210

Prilleltensky, I. (2008). "The role of power in wellness, oppression, and liberation: The promise of psychopolitical validity". *Journal of Community Psychology*, 36(2), 116–136. https://doi.org/10.1002/jcop.20225

Putnam, R. D. (2000). *Bowling Alone: The Collapse and Revival of American Community*. Simon & Schuster.

Rank, M. R. (2004). *One Nation, Underprivileged: Why American Poverty Affects Us All*. Oxford University Press.

Rappaport, J. (1987). "Terms of empowerment/exemplars of prevention: Toward a theory for community psychology". *American Journal of Community Psychology*, 15(2), 121–148. https://doi.org/10.1007/BF00919275

Raymond, C., Marin, M. F., Hand, A., Sindi, S., Juster, R. P., & Lupien, S. J. (2016). "Salivary Cortisol Levels and Depressive Symptomatology in Consumers and Nonconsumers of Self-Help Books: A Pilot Study". *Neural Plasticity*, 2016(1), 3136743.

Rhode, D. L. (1996). "Myths of meritocracy". *Fordham L. Rev.*, 65, 585.

Riemer, M., Reich, S. M., Evans, S. D., Nelson, G., & Prilleltensky, I. (Eds.). (2020). *Community Psychology: In Pursuit of Liberation and Wellbeing*. Bloomsbury Publishing.

Rimke, H. M. (2000). "Governing Citizens Through Self-Help Literature". *Cultural Studies*, 14(1), 61–78.

Rogers, C. R. (1961). *On Becoming a Person: A Therapist's View of Psychotherapy*. London: Constable, p. 0.

Rosen, G. M. (1993). "Self-help or hype? Comments on psychology's failure to advance self-care". *Professional Psychology: Research and Practice*, 24(3), 340.

Rosen, G. M., Glasgow, R. E., & Moore, T. E. (2003). Self-help therapy: The science and business of giving psychology away. In S. O. Lilienfeld, S. J. Lynn, & J. M. Lohr (Eds.), Science and pseudoscience in clinical psychology (pp. 399–424). The Guilford Press.

Rosenberg, M., & McCullough, B. C. (1981). "Mattering: Inferred significance and mental health among adolescents". *Research in Community and Mental Health*, 2, 163–182.

Rousseau, J.-J. (1762). *The Social Contract*. (G. D. H. Cole, Trans.).

Rosen, G. M. (1993). "Self-help or hype? Comments on psychology's failure to advance self-care". *Professional Psychology: Research and Practice*, 24(3), 340.

Ryan, W. (2010). *Blaming the Victim*. Vintage.

Salerno, S. (2006). *SHAM: How the Self-Help Movement Made America Helpless*. Forum Books.

Sampson, R. J., Raudenbush, S. W., & Earls, F. (1997). "Neighborhoods and violent crime: A multilevel study of collective efficacy". *Science*, 277(5328), 918–924. https://doi.org/10.1126/science.277.5328.918

Sandberg, S. (2014). *Lean In*. Random House.

Shafran, R., & Rachman, S. (2004). "Thought-action fusion: a review". *Journal of Behavior Therapy and Experimental Psychiatry*, 35(2), 87–107.

Sheldon, K. M., Kashdan, T. B., & Steger, M. F. (Eds.). (2011). *Designing Positive Psychology: Taking Stock and Moving Forward*. Oxford University Press.

Sincero, J. (2013). *You Are a Badass: How to Stop Doubting Your Greatness and Start Living an Awesome Life*. Running Press.

Skinner, B. F. (1948). "Superstition in the pigeon". *Journal of Experimental Psychology*, 38(2), 168.

Smallwood, J., & Schooler, J. W. (2015). "The science of mind wandering: Empirically navigating the stream of consciousness". *Annual Review of psychology*, 66(1), 487–518.

Smiles, S. (1866). *Self-Help with Illustrations of Character and Conduct*. John Murray.

Snyder, C. R. (2002). "Hope theory: Rainbows in the mind". *Psychological Inquiry*, 13(4), 249–275.

Soss, J., Fording, R. C., & Schram, S. F. (2011). *Disciplining the Poor: Neoliberal Paternalism and the Persistent Power of Race*. University of Chicago Press.

Standing, G. (2015). "The precariat and class struggle". RCCS Annual Review. A selection from the Portuguese journal *Revista Crítica de Ciências Sociais*, (7).

Steger, M. F., Dik, B. J., & Duffy, R. D. (2012). "Meaningful work: Connecting the realms of work and spirituality". *American Psychological Association*.

Stoeber, J., & Childs, J. H. (2011). Perfectionism. In R. J. R. Levesque (Ed.), Encyclopedia of adolescence (pp. 2053–2059). New York: Springer. DOI: 10.1007/978-1-4419-1695-2_279

Spence, G. B., Cavanagh, M. J., & Grant, A. M. (2008). "The integration of mindfulness training and health coaching:

An exploratory study". *Coaching: An International Journal of Theory, Research and Practice*, 1(2), 145–163.

Starker, S. (2002). *Oracle at the Supermarket: The American Preoccupation with Self-Help Books*. Transaction Publishers.

Tajfel, H., & Turner, J. C. (1986). "The social identity theory of intergroup behavior". In S. Worchel & W. G. Austin (Eds.), *Psychology of Intergroup Relations* (pp. 7–24). Nelson-Hall.

Tarrow, S. (2011). *Power in Movement: Social Movements and Contentious Politics* (3rd ed.). Cambridge University Press.

Tavris, C. (2014). *Science and Pseudoscience in Clinical Psychology*. Guilford Publications.

Taylor, J., & Turner, R. J. (2001). "A longitudinal study of the role and significance of mattering to others for depressive symptoms". *Journal of Health and Social Behavior*, 42(3), 310–325. https://doi.org/10.2307/3090217

The Business Research Company (2024) The Personal Growth Market Report [Accessed 09/08/2024] https://www.thebusinessresearchcompany.com/report/personal-development-global-market-report#:~:text=The%20personal%20development%20market%20size,(CAGR)%20of%206.1%25.

Tough, P. (2008). *Whatever It Takes: Geoffrey Canada's Quest to Change Harlem and America*. Houghton Mifflin Harcourt.

Tourish, D., & Vatcha, N. (2005). "Charismatic leadership and corporate cultism at Enron: The elimination of dissent, the promotion of conformity and organizational collapse". *Leadership*, 1(4), 455–480.

Triandis, H. C. (1995). *Individualism and Collectivism*. Westview Press.

Turkle, S. (2011). *Alone Together: Why We Expect More from Technology and Less from Each Other*. Basic Books.

Uchino, B. N. (2009). "Understanding the links between social support and physical health: A life-span perspective with emphasis on the separability of perceived and received support". *Perspectives on Psychological Science*, 4(3), 236–255. https://doi.org/10.1111/j.1745-6924.2009.01122.x

Verdonk, P., & Houkes, I. (2010). *Bright-Sided. How the Relentless Promotion of Positive Thinking Has Undermined America.* Gedrag & Organisatie, 23(2).

Victora, C. G., Barreto, M. L., Leal, M. C., Monteiro, C. A., Schmidt, M. I., Paim, J., & Do Carmo Leal, M. (2011). "Health conditions and health-policy innovations in Brazil: The way forward". *The Lancet*, 377(9782), 2042–2053. https://doi.org/10.1016/S0140-6736(11)60055-X

Wacquant, L., & Wacquant, L. (2020). *Punishing the Poor: The Neoliberal Government of Social Insecurity.* Duke University Press.

Walker, M. (2017). *Why We Sleep: Unlocking the Power of Sleep and Dreams.* Simon and Schuster.

Wandersman, A., & Florin, P. (2003). "Community interventions and effective prevention". *American Psychologist*, 58(6–7), 441.

Wampler, B. (2007). *Participatory Budgeting in Brazil: Contestation, Cooperation, and Accountability.* Penn State Press.

Wampler, B. (2007). "Participatory Budgeting in Brazil: Contestation, Cooperation, and Accountability". *Latin American Politics and Society*, 49(2), 1–26. https://doi.org/10.1111/j.1548-2456.2007.tb00378.x

Weber, M., & Kalberg, S. (2013). *The Protestant Ethic and the Spirit of Capitalism.* Routledge.

Wilkinson, R., & Pickett, K. (2011). *The Spirit Level: Why Greater Equality Makes Societies Stronger.* Bloomsbury Publishing USA

World Health Organization. (2019). Burn-out an "occupational phenomenon": *International classification of diseases.* Accessed from https://www.who.int/mental_health/evidence/burn-out/en/

## Framespotting
Changing how you look at things changes how you see them
Laurence & Alison Matthews
A punchy, upbeat guide to framespotting. Spot deceptions
and hidden assumptions; swap growth for growing up.
See and be free.
Paperback: 978-1-78279-689-3 ebook: 978-1-78279-822-4

## Is There an Afterlife?
David Fontana
Is there an Afterlife? If so what is it like? How do
Western ideas of the afterlife compare with Eastern?
David Fontana presents the historical and contemporary
evidence for survival of physical death.
Paperback: 978-1-90381-690-5

## Nothing Matters
a book about nothing
Ronald Green
Thinking about Nothing opens the world to
everything by illuminating new angles to old problems
and stimulating new ways of thinking.
Paperback: 978-1-84694-707-0 ebook: 978-1-78099-016-3

## Panpsychism
The Philosophy of the Sensuous Cosmos
Peter Ells
Are free will and mind chimeras? This book, anti-
materialistic but respecting science, answers: No!
Mind is foundational to all existence.
Paperback: 978-1-84694-505-2 ebook: 978-1-78099-018-7

## Punk Science
Inside the Mind of God
Manjir Samanta-Laughton
Many have experienced unexplainable phenomena; God,
psychic abilities, extraordinary healing and angelic encounters.
Can cutting-edge science actually explain phenomena
previously thought of as 'paranormal'?
Paperback: 978-1-90504-793-2

## The Vagabond Spirit of Poetry
Edward Clarke
Spend time with the wisest poets of the modern age and
of the past, and let Edward Clarke remind you of the
importance of poetry in our industrialized world.
Paperback: 978-1-78279-370-0 ebook: 978-1-78279-369-4


Readers of ebooks can buy or view any of these bestsellers by
clicking on the live link in the title. Most titles are published in
paperback and as an ebook. Paperbacks are available in traditional
bookshops. Both print and ebook formats are available online.
Find more titles and sign up to our readers' newsletter at
www.collectiveinkbooks.com/non-fiction
Follow us on Facebook at
www.facebook.com/CINonFiction